THE STATE
Hermitage

Guidebook

P-2 ART PUBLISHERS

ST PETERSBURG, 2010

THE STATE
Hermitage

Text by SOPHIA KUDRIAVTSEVA

Photographs by VALENTIN BARANOVSKY, PAVEL DEMIDOV, VLADIMIR DENISOV,
LEONARD KHEIFETS, VLADIMIR MELNIKOV, YURY MOLODKOVETS,
ALEXANDER PETROSIAN, VIKTOR SAVIK, EVGUENY SINIAVER,
VLADIMIR TEREBENIN, OLEG TRUBSKY AND VASILY VORONTSOV

Edited by IRINA KHARITONOVA AND IRINA LVOVA

Translated by JULIA REDKINA

Colour correction by VIACHESLAV BYKOVSKI, VLADIMIR KNIAZEV
 AND ALEXANDER MIAGKOV

P-2 Art Publishers, 3, Ulitsa Mira, St Petersburg, Russia 197101

CONTENTS

The State Hermitage ranks among the greatest museums in the world. Its universal and national value makes it a most significant object of the Russian Federation cultural heritage.

The pride of the museum is the architectural complex where its collections are displayed. It has been formed in the cause of almost a century and a half in the very heart of St Petersburg. The world-famous assemblage of art works held in the Hermitage provides a unique status of the museum both as national and international cul-

View of the State Hermitage complex of buildings

tural space. Its attractiveness is much contributed to by its eventful past inextricably linked with the birth, heyday and decline of St Petersburg as the capital of the Russian Empire.

On entering the museum visitors find themselves in majestic exhibition rooms displaying thousands of art works, which are at the same time exquisitely designed architectural interiors and unique historical sites.

Palace Square Ensemble

Palace Square got its name in the middle of the 18th century when the Winter Palace, main Imperial residence, was constructed on the bank of the River Neva. The well-balanced composition of the square was designed in 1819−29 by Carlo Rossi who united the royal palace and the General Staff building, constructed under his supervision in 1819−23, into an integral architectural ensemble. Later the ensemble was completed by the granite Alexander Column and the Staff of the Guards Corps (architect Alexander Briullov).

Railing of the Winter Palace's Main Gate

Portico of the New Hermitage

St Petersburg consists of a long chain of squares connected with one another. Thus the Field of Mars is joined to Palace Square by Millionnaya Street running along the New Hermitage facade. Its main entrance adorned with a portico supported by ten huge statues serves as sort of introduction to Palace Square. The statues of Atlantes carved from Serdobol granite at the workshop of the sculptor Alexander Terebenev in 1844−49 are not only traditionally associated with Palace Square and the Hermitage but also well known as a highlight emblematic of St Petersburg.

The Alexander Column standing in the centre of the square impresses everyone with its elegant proportions, majestic silhouette and refined lines. Designed by Au-

Palace Square. The Winter Palace and the Alexander Column

guste de Montferrand, it was erected in 1834 to commemorate Russia's victory in the Patriotic War of 1812 against Napoleon. This tallest in the world column (47.5 m) made of a single monolith is named after Emperor Alexander I in whose reign the war with Napoleon was won. The face of the angel crowning the column was made by Boris Orlovsky to resemble that of the emperor. The heavenly messenger trampling upon a snake is an allegory of peace granted to Europe by Russia after its victory over Napoleonic France. The stone block of the column (its weight is 600 tons, or 1, 322, 760 pounds) has no attachment to the base, neither is it dug into the soil – it stands by its own weight thanks to the precise calculations of the architect.

Angel atop the Alexander Column

Chariot of Victory crowning the General Staff building

Palace Square. The General Staff building and the Alexander Column

Great Courtyard

Detail of the Main Gate railing

Great Courtyard of the Winter Palace

Since the time of its creation, the Great Courtyard, of about 11, 000 m², had been serving as main entrance to the Winter Palace. After the Revolution of 1917 it ceased to play its ceremonial role. In May 2003, when the 300th anniversary of St Petersburg's foundation was celebrated, the reconstructed courtyard was reopened for the public.

The large rectangle of the courtyard framed by the gorgeous Winter Palace, designed by Francesco Bartolomeo Rastrelli, is a prelude not only to the palace but also to the entire museum complex. During the White Nights this unique "green vestibule" becomes a venue for concerts and performances given in the open air.

Main Gate

Double-headed eagle
crowning the Main Gate

A bird's eye view of the Great Courtyard

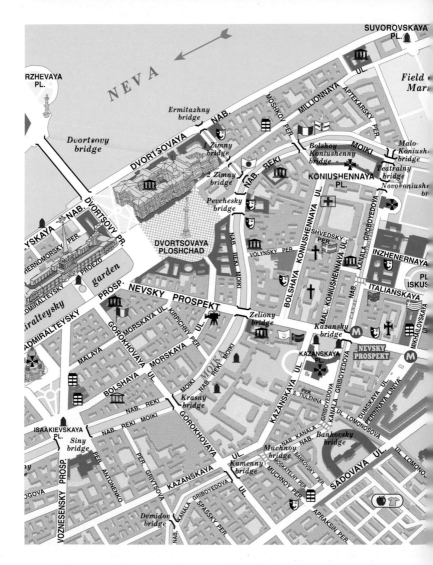

Information

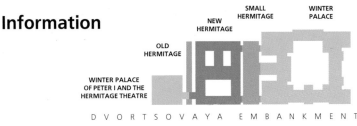

SMALL HERMITAGE

WINTER PALACE

NEW HERMITAGE

OLD HERMITAGE

WINTER PALACE OF PETER I AND THE HERMITAGE THEATRE

D V O R T S O V A Y A   E M B A N K M E N T

The State Hermitage Museum Complex

HOW TO GET THERE
Metro stations: Gostiny Dvor and Nevsky Prospekt; trolleybuses 1, 7, 10 and 11; buses 7 and 24

OPENING HOURS
Tuesday – Saturday: 10.30 – 18.00
Sunday: 10.30 – 17.00
Closed on Monday
The ticket office closes an hour before the museum's closing time.
Entrance from Dvortsovaya (Palace) Square

TEMPORARY EXHIBITIONS
Temporary exhibitions are closed half an hour before the museum's closing time.
Photography and filming is forbidden at temporary exhibitions.

INFORMATION
There is an information desk in the Main Vestibule. Its staff will answer all your questions about the museum and offer you museum floor plans and booklets about temporary exhibitions.

NAVIGATION KIOSKS
Sited by the Main Staircase, these computer kiosks help visitors find their way round the museum. The chosen route can be printed out.

TELEPHONE INFORMATION
(007) (812) 571-3420, (007) (812) 571-9625 and 089

INTERNET ADDRESS
www.hermitagemuseum.org

GUIDED TOURS
Entrance from Dvortsovaya (Palace) Square through the Main Gate arch
General and specialized tours in Russian and foreign languages can be booked at the Hermitage Tour Office.
Bookings: (007) (812) 571-8446

AUDIOGUIDES
Main Gallery, 1st floor and landing of the Main Staircase, 2nd floor
Audioguides are available in Russian, English, French and German.

TREASURE GALLERY 1 AND 2
These galleries can be visited only on a timed guided tour. Tour times are displayed on the board in the Main Vestibule. Bookings can be made at the Hermitage Tour Office. Bookings: (007) (812) 571-8446

MUSEUM SHOP
Rastrelli Gallery, Commandant Entrance, 1st floor and landing of the Main Staircase, 2nd floor
It offers a variety of printed materials and souvenirs. Opening hours are as for the museum.

CAFE
Rastrelli Gallery, 1st floor

MULTIMEDIA EDUCATION CENTRE
Rastrelli Gallery, 1st floor
It offers multimedia programmes featuring various aspects of the museum's collections.

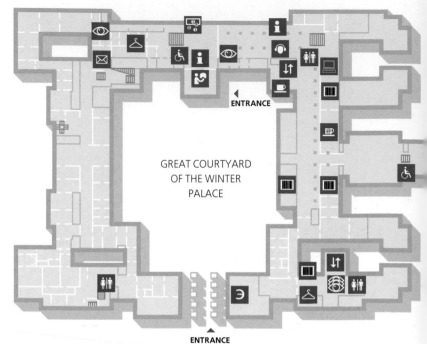

ENTRANCE

GREAT COURTYARD
OF THE WINTER
PALACE

ENTRANCE

D V O R T S O V A Y A (P A L A C E) S Q U A R E

LECTURES
For adults:
(007) (812) 710-9731
For schoolchildren:
(007) (812) 710-9551

VISITING RULES
Please, do not bring any
large items into the museum.
Bags, cases, rucksacks,
umbrellas etc. must be left
in the cloakrooms.
Photography and video
recordings are permitted
only on purchase of a special
ticket.
Please, do not speak over
the mobile phone in the
museum.

**ACCESS FOR VISITORS
WITH LIMITED MOBILITY**
Entrance from Dvortsovaya
(Palace) Square
To arrange access for visitors
with special needs or in
wheelchairs, please, contact
the Administrator in the
Main Vestibule or call (007)
(812) 710-9079

HERMITAGE FRIENDS CLUB
The Club Office is located by
the Commandant Entrance
of the Winter Palace. Club
representatives are also to
be found at desks in the
Main Vestibule and at the
Commandant Entrance. For
further information about
the club: (007) (812) 710-
9005; fax: (007) (812) 571-
9528; email: development@
hermitage.ru

TOILETS
Main Staircase,
Commandant Entrance,
Council (Sovetskaya)
Staircase, Terebenev
Staircase and cloakrooms

S I G N S

TICKET SALES

INFORMATION POINT

CLOAKROOM

ENTRANCE TO GALLERIES

ENTRANCE TO GALLERIES
FOR GROUPS

INVALID ACCESS

ATM/CASH POINT

LIFT

AUDIOGUIDE RENTAL

TOILETS

CAFE

INTERNET CAFE

MUSEUM SHOP

MULTIMEDIA EDUCATION
CENTRE

TOUR OFFICE

POST OFFICE

Branches of the State Hermitage

THE WINTER PALACE OF PETER I

32 Dvortsovaya (Palace) Embankment

This palace (architects Georg Mattarnovi and Domenico Trezzini) once stood on the site of the Hermitage Theatre. In 1720−22 it was the official royal residence. Today the surviving part of the palace is occupied by a commemorative exhibition dedicated to Peter the Great and his epoch.

THE GENERAL STAFF

6−8 Dvortsovaya (Palace) Square

The General Staff was built in 1820−27 to a design of Carlo Rossi. It is an outstanding example of Russian Neoclassicism. The eastern wing, formerly home to the Ministries of Foreign Affairs and Finance of the Russian Empire, houses the Guards Museum and other permanent and temporary exhibitions of the State Hermitage.

THE MENSHIKOV PALACE

15 University Embankment

The palace of Alexander Menshikov, the first governor of St Petersburg, is one of very few surviving buildings from the epoch of Peter I. It was put up in 1710−11 to a design of Giovanni Mario Fontana and Gottfried Schaedel. Today the palace is part of the State Hermitage Museum housing the exhibition *Russian Culture of the First Third of the 18th Century*.

STATE HERMITAGE RESTORATION AND STORAGE CENTRE

37a Zausadebnaya Street

The modern storage facility equipped to meet the up-to-date museum standards was opened to the public in 2004. It can be visited with a guided tour that presents extensive collections of furniture, carriages and other items which for many years have been inaccessible for the wide public.

THE MUSEUM OF PORCELAIN

151 Prospekt Obukhovskoy Oborony (On the territory of the Imperial Porcelain Factory)

Founded in 1844, the museum was originally part of the Imperial Porcelain Factory. Since 2001 it has been a branch of the State Hermitage. Its collection comprises more than 30, 000 items, works produced by the Imperial Porcelain Factory and glass and porcelain from leading European and Russian manufactories of the 18th − 20th centuries.

Plans of State Rooms and Collections

State Rooms of the 2nd floor
ILLUSTRATIONS SHOW MOST NOTEWORTHY ROOMS

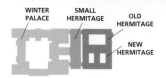

WINTER PALACE SMALL HERMITAGE OLD HERMITAGE NEW HERMITAGE

DVORTSOVAYA (PALACE) SQUARE

191 LARGE NICHOLAS HALL (p. 48)

192 ANTEROOM (p. 46)

Peter I (Small Throne) Room

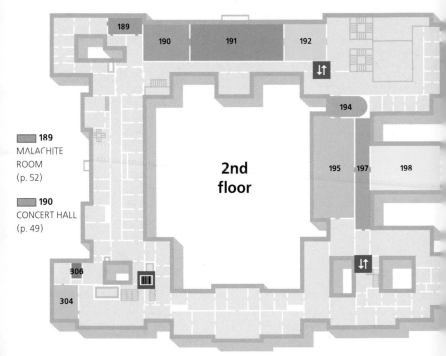

189 MALACHITE ROOM (p. 52)

190 CONCERT HALL (p. 49)

2nd floor

Golden Dwelling Room

306 BOUDOIR (p. 51)

304 GOLDEN DWELLING ROOM (p. 50)

St George (Large Throne) Hall

1812 War Gallery

Pavilion Hall

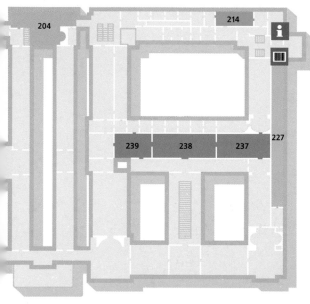

**Leonardo
da Vinci Room**

Large Italian Skylight Hall

Raphael Loggias

Collections of the 1st floor
ILLUSTRATIONS SHOW HIGHLIGHTS OF THE MUSEUM COLLECTIONS

WINTER PALACE
SMALL HERMITAGE
OLD HERMITAGE
NEW HERMITAGE

DVORTSOVAYA (PALACE) SQUARE

Statue of Amenemhat III. 19th century BC

Collections of the Winter Palace

11–33 ARCHAEOLOGY OF EASTERN EUROPE AND SIBERIA (p. 142)

89–91, 100 ART OF ANCIENT EGYPT AND ASIA MINOR (p. 120)

Idol of Galich. Second half of the 2nd millennium BC

1st floor

Plaque: *Deer.* Early 6th century BC

Feasting Man. Fragment of mural painting. First half of the 8th century

TREASURE GALLERY 2 (p. 148)

46–52, 55–63, 66, 68, 69 ART OF CENTRAL ASIA AND THE CAUCASUS (p. 124)

Collections of the Old and New Hermitage

▬▬▬ 101, 102, 106–117, 121, 127–131
ART OF ANTIQUITY
(p. 270)

▬▬▬
TREASURE
GALLERY 1
(p. 278)

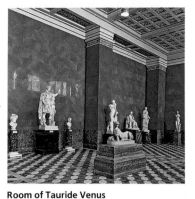

Room of Tauride Venus

Statue of Emperor Octavian Augustus shown as Jupiter. First half of the 1st century

Portraits of Ptolemy II and Arsinoe II (Gonzaga Cameo). 3rd century BC

Bouquet of Flowers. 1840s. By Jeremie Pauzier

Hall of Jupiter

Aphrodite (Tauride Venus). 3rd century BC

Collections of the 2nd floor
ILLUSTRATIONS SHOW HIGHLIGHTS OF THE MUSEUM COLLECTIONS

WINTER PALACE • SMALL HERMITAGE • OLD HERMITAGE • NEW HERMITAGE

DVORTSOVAYA (PALACE) SQUARE

Bartolomeo Carlo Rastrelli. *Sculptural Portrait of Peter I.* 1723–29

Collections of the Small Hermitage

▭ **259**
WESTERN EUROPEAN APPLIED ART OF THE MIDDLE AGES (p. 158)

2nd floor

Collections of the Winter Palace

▭ **147–151, 153, 155–190**
RUSSIAN CULTURE: 9th – 19th CENTURIES (p. 108)

▭ **298–301**
BRITISH ART: 16th – 19th CENTURIES (c. 70)

▭ **272–297**
FRENCH ART: 15th – 18th CENTURIES (p. 56)

Antoine Watteau. *Capricious Woman.* Circa 1780

▭ **258, 261, 262**
NETHERLANDISH ART: 15th – 16th CENTURIES (p. 162)

▭ **255–257**
GERMAN ART: 15th – 20th CENTURIES (p. 172)

Pieter Paul Rubens. *The Union of Earth and Water.* Early 1620s

Leonardo da Vinci.
Madonna and Child (Litta Madonna).
1470 – circa 1490/91

Collections of the Old and New Hermitage

▨ **207–223, 227, 229–238**
ITALIAN ART:
14th – 18th CENTURIES
(p. 190, 226)

▨ **239–240**
SPANISH ART:
15th – 19th CENTURIES
(p. 236)

▨ **249–254**
DUTCH ART:
17th – 18th CENTURIES
(p. 254)

▨ **245–248**
FLEMISH ART:
17th – 18th CENTURIES (p. 246)

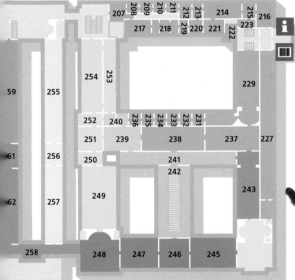

Antonio Canova.
The Three Graces. 1813

Rembrandt. *The Return of the Prodigal Son.* Circa 1668–69

▨ **243**
WESTERN EUROPEAN ARMS AND ARMOUR:
15th – 17th CENTURIES (p. 264)

▨ **241**
GALLERY OF THE HISTORY OF ANCIENT PAINTING
(p. 220)

▨ **242**
STATE STAIRCASE
(p. 214)

Collections of the 3rd floor
ILLUSTRATIONS SHOW HIGHLIGHTS OF THE MUSEUM COLLECTIONS

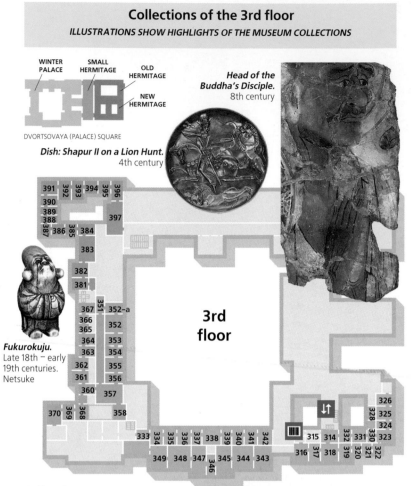

WINTER PALACE   SMALL HERMITAGE   OLD HERMITAGE

NEW HERMITAGE

DVORTSOVAYA (PALACE) SQUARE

Head of the Buddha's Disciple. 8th century

Dish: Shapur II on a Lion Hunt. 4th century

3rd floor

Fukurokuju. Late 18th – early 19th centuries. Netsuke

Collections of the Winter Palace

▭ **381–397** BYZANTINE ART AND ART OF THE NEAR EAST (p. 128)

▭ **351–370** ART OF THE FAR EAST (p. 134)

▭ **314, 316–326, 333–350** FRENCH ART AND ART OF OTHER WESTERN EUROPEAN COUNTRIES: 19th – 20Th CENTURIES (p. 80)

Eugene Delacroix. *Lion Hunt in Morocco.* 1854

Auguste Rodin. *Eternal Spring.* Early 1900s

Impressionists and Post-Impressionists

Claude Monet. *Lady in the Garden.* 1867

Edgar Degas. *Woman Combing Her Hair.* 1885–86

Pierre-Auguste Renoir. *Girl with a Fan.* 1881

Paul Cezanne. *Mont Sainte-Victoire.* 1900

Vincent van Gogh. *Ladies of Arles.* 1888

Paul Gauguin. *Woman Holding a Fruit.* 1893

Pablo Picasso. *Woman with a Fan.* 1908

Henri Matisse. *The Red Room.* 1908

Chronicle of the Imperial Hermitage

Empress Elizabeth Petrovna. 1709–1761

Empress Catherine II. 1729–1796

Elizabeth Petrovna

1754–61 Construction of the Winter Palace (architect Francesco Bartolomeo Rastrelli)

Catherine II

1762 The Winter Palace became the residence of the Russian emperors and empresses

1764 Purchase of Johann Ernest Gotzkowski's collection (paintings by Dutch and Flemish artists including Rembrandt's *Doubting Thomas*, *Portrait of a Young Man with a Glove* by Frans Hals, Jacob Jordaens' *Family Portrait* and the *Revellers* by Jan Steen)

1764–65 Construction of the Southern Pavilion, Hanging Garden and Manege in the Small Hermitage (architect Yury Velten)

1766 Purchase of Rembrandt's *Return of the Prodigal Son*

1767 Purchase of J. de Jullienne's collection (paintings by Dutch and Flemish artists including *Peasant Wedding* by David Teniers II, Gabriel Metsu's *Doctor's Visit* and *Study of a Cat's Head* by Frans Snyders)

1767–69 Construction of the Northern Pavilion of the Small Hermitage (architect Vallin de la Mothe)

1769 Purchase of Count Heinrich von Bruhl's collection (paintings by Dutch, Flemish, French, Italian and German artists including *Perseus and Andromeda* and *Landscape with a Rainbow* by Pieter Paul Rubens, Antoine Watteau's *Holy Family* and *Embarrassing Proposal*, Nicolas Poussin's *Descent from the Cross*, Rembrandt's *Portrait of a Scholar*, *Maecenas Presenting the Liberal Arts to Emperor Augustus* by Giovanni Battista Tiepolo and Lucas Cranach's

Venus and Cupid)

1771–75 Construction of the western part of the Old (Large) Hermitage, with its Oval and Small Rooms, Rotunda, Bedroom and a small theatre (architect Yury Velten)

1772 Purchase of Baron Pierre Crozat's collection. It included such masterpieces as Raphael's *Holy Family*, Giorgione's *Judith*, a *Danae* by Titian, *Danae* and the *Holy Family* by Rembrandt and a *Pieta* by Paolo Veronese. Two canvases by Pieter Paul Rubens were also acquired; these were *Bacchus* and *Portrait of a Lady-in-Waiting to the Infanta Isabella*, as well as his sketches for the Luxembourg Palace in Paris and other works. Anthony van Dyck was represented by six portraits, including his *Self-Portrait*. Along with paintings from the Italian, Flemish, Dutch and Netherlandish schools the collection of

Crozat was rich in works by French artists of the 17th and 18th centuries such as Louis Le Nain, Nicolas Poussin, Pierre Mignard, Nicolas de Largillierre, Antoine Watteau (*Actors of the Comedie Francaise*), Nicolas Lancret and Jean-Baptiste Simeon Chardin (*Washerwoman*)

1774 Issue of the first Hermitage Catalogue (in French)

1775 Construction of the Western and Eastern Galleries running along the Hanging Garden of the Small Hermitage (architect Yury Velten)

1777–87 Construction of the eastern part of the Old (Large) Hermitage, decoration and furnishing of its interiors (architect Yury Velten)

1779 Purchase of Sir Robert Walpole's collection. The Hermitage gained such remarkable works as *Bacchus* and *Vulcan's Forge* by Luca Giordano, Guido Reni's *Fathers of the Church Disputing*, Salvator Rosa's *Prodigal Son* and *Democritus and Protagoras* and other canvases that formed the bulk of the Hermitage collection of 17th-century Italian painting. The collection of Flemish art was considerably enriched and that section of the picture gallery now remains essentially the same as it was then: it received Rubens's *Stone Carters* and *Feast in the House of Simon the Pharisee*, along with many of the works by Anthony van Dyck (such as the *Madonna with Partridges* and portraits from his London period); there were four enormous canvases from the *Stalls* series and *Birds' Concert*, all by Frans Snyders. The other artistic schools were not neglected, with the *Holy Family* and *Moses Striking the Rock* by Nicolas Poussin, the *Immaculate Conception* and the *Adoration of the Shepherds* by Bartolome Esteban Murillo and the *Sacrifice of Isaac* by Rembrandt Harmenszoon van Rijn

1781 Purchase of Count Baudouin's collection, with its first-rate paintings, mainly from the Dutch and Flemish schools. This was the last major addition to the Hermitage gallery in the 18th century. It comprised nine works by Rembrandt (*Portrait of an Old Man*, *Portrait of an Old Woman* and *Portrait of the Poet Jeremias de Decker*) and paintings by Anthony van Dyck, Adriaen van Ostade, Jacob van Ruysdael and David Teniers II

1783–89 Construction of the Hermitage Theatre (architect Giacomo Quarenghi)

1783–92 Creation of the Raphael Loggias (architect Giacomo Quarenghi)

1785 First performance given at the Hermitage Theatre

1786 First repair of the Winter Palace facades

1787 Purchase of John Lyde-Brown's collection. The most valuable items are an early Greek sculptural portrait, known as likeness of Gaius Servilius Ahala, Roman busts of Emperor Lucius Verus and Cornelia Salonina and a model for the equestrian statue of Louis XIV by Francois Girardon

1787–88 Installation of the Vatican paintings' copies in the Raphael Loggias

1788–93 Reconstruction of the north-western part of the Winter Palace (architect Antonio Rinaldi) in connection with the wedding of Grand Duke Alexander Pavlovich

1791 Redecoration of the Grand Duke and Grand Duchess apartments (architect Giacomo Quarenghi) in the Winter Palace

1791–93 Creation of the Neva Suite of state rooms comprising the Anteroom, Large Anteroom (since 1856 Nicholas Hall) and Concert Hall (architect Giacomo Quarenghi) in the Winter Palace

1795 Ceremonial opening of the St George (Large Throne) Hall (architect Giacomo Quarenghi) in the Winter Palace. Installation of sloping ways (architects Giacomo Quarenghi and Ivan Starov) in the Winter Palace and Small Hermitage providing access for the carriage of Catherine II

Alexander I

1801–16 Creation of the apartments of Emperor Alexander I and Empress Elizaveta Alexeyevna (architect Luiggi Rusca) in the Winter Palace

1804–07 Reconstruction of the Eastern Picture Gallery in the Small Hermitage (architect Giacomo Quarenghi)

1805–07 Reconstruction of the Main Suite of state rooms in the Old (Large) Hermitage (architect Giacomo Quarenghi)

Emperor Alexander I. 1777–1825

1814–15 Purchase of Baron William Coesvelt's collection of the Spanish school which had a few canvases by Fracisco Ribalta, *Still Life* by Antonio Pereda, Antonio de Puga's *Knife Grinder* and *Portrait of Count-Duke Olivares* by Diego Velazquez

1815 Purchase of Empress Josephine's collection housed in her Malmaison Palace. The Hermitage was enriched by the *Holy Family* by Andrea del Sarto, two paintings of the *Descent from the Cross* by Rembrandt and Rubens, a series devoted to the different times of the day by Claude Lorrain, Gerard Terborch's *A Glass of Lemonade*, Gabriel Metsu's Breakfast and the *Farm* by Paulus Potter. Important for the Hermitage was the acquisition of four sculptures by Antonio Canova: *Hebe, Paris, Dancer* and *Cupid and Psyche*

1825 Creation of an exhibition featuring Russian art

Emperor Nicholas I.
1796–1855

Nicholas I

1826 Creation of the 1812 War Gallery (architect Carlo Rossi) in the Winter Palace

1827–28 Redecoration of the apartments of Empress Maria Fyodorovna (architects Carlo Rossi and Auguste de Montferrand) in the Winter Palace

1830 Reconstruction of the Concert Hall (architect Auguste de Montferrand) in the Winter Palace

1833 Creation of the Field Marshals and Peter I Rooms (architect Auguste de Montferrand) in the Winter Palace

1837 Fire in the Winter Palace

1837–39 Restoration of Rastrelli's Main (Jordan) Staircase by the architect Vasily Stasov in the Winter Palace. Restoration of the Neva and Main Suites of state rooms, Grand and Small churches (architect Vasily Stasov) in the Winter Palace. Creation of the Malachite Room (architect Alexander Briullov) in the Winter Palace

1838–41 Restoration of the 1812 War Gallery and St George Hall (architect Vasily Stasov) in the Winter Palace

1839–41 Creation of the White Dwelling Room, Golden Dwelling Room, Crimson Study and other interiors (architect Alexander Briullov) in the so-called New Apartments of the Heir Apparent in the Winter Palace

1840s Reconstruction of the Small Hermitage (architects Vasily Stasov and Nikolai Yefimov)

1840–44 Reconstruction of the Hanging Garden, Romanov and Peter I galleries and Southern Pavilion (architects Vasily Stasov and Nikolai Yefimov) in the Small Hermitage

1842–51 Construction of the New Hermitage (to a design by Leo von Klenze

Emperor Alexander II.
1818–1881

under supervision of Vasily Stasov and Nikolai Yefimov)

1850s Finishing of the interiors of the so-called New Apartments of the Heir Apparent (architect Andrei Stakenschneider) in the Winter Palace

1850 Purchase of Cristoforo Barbarigo's collection. The Hermitage gained five paintings by Titian, including his masterpieces – the *Repentant Mary Magdalene* and *St Sebastian*

1850–58 Reconstruction of the Northern Pavilion of the Small Hermitage; creation of the Pavilion Hall on the site of the former "greenhouse" (architect Andrei Stakenschneider)

1851–52 Installation of a copy of the floor mosaics, unearthed in the Ancient Roman bath at Ocriculum, in the Pavilion Hall of the Small Hermitage

1851–60 Redecoration of the Main Suite of state rooms (architect Andrei Stakenschneider) in the Old (Large) Hermitage

1852 Opening of the Imperial Museum of the New Hermitage

1853 Reconstruction of the Boudoir of Empress Maria Alexandrovna (architect Harold Bosse) in the Winter Palace

Alexander II

1859 Transfer of Peter I's Siberian collection from the Kunstkammer (Chamber of Curiosities) to the Hermitage

1861 Purchase of Marquis Giampietro Campana's collection. Some items purchased became highlights of the Hermitage collection, such as ancient sculptural portraits, statues of the nine muses, an enormous statue of Jupiter and a relief showing the death of Niobe's children. Also noteworthy are Etruscan items, Italic and Attic vases and bronzes including the famous "Regina Vasorum", or "Queen of Vases", plus frescoes by Raphael's apprentices

1865 Acquisition of Leonardo da Vinci's *Litta Madonna*

1870 Acquisition of Raphael's *Conestabile Madonna*

1880–90 Installation of electricity in the Winter Palace

Alexander III

1883–88 Reconstruction of the palace stables and Manege

1884–86 Purchase of Alexander Basilewski's collection. Well represented in it was early Christian and Byzantine art, as well as church plate from the Romanesque and Gothic periods, ivories of the 13th and 14th centuries, enamels from the Rhine area and Limoges dating from the 12th to 16th century, Venetian and German glass, Italian majolica, French and Spanish-Moorish faience Creation of the railing of the Winter Palace's Main Gate

and decoration of its Great Courtyard (architects Nikolai Gornostayev and Fyodor Melzer)

1885 Transfer to the Hermitage of the Imperial Arsenal collection from Tsarskoye Selo

1888 Repair of the Winter Palace facades

1890s Decoration of the apartments for the Heir Apparent Nicholas Alexandrovich and his wife Alexandra Fyodorovna (architect Alexander Krasovsky)

1893–94 Sculptures on the roofs of the Winter Palace were replaced with statues made after the models of Mikhail Popov

1893–95 Reconstruction of the Hanging Garden terrace (architect Alexander Krasovsky)

Nicholas II

Late 19th – early 20th centuries Gold objects from the Scythian barrows were

Emperor Alexander III.
1845–1894

Emperor Nicholas II.
1868–1918

added to the collection

1896–1901 A garden (designed by Nikolai Kramskoi) was laid out by the Winter Palace on the Admiralty side and a railing (designed by Fyodor Melzer) was set up around it

1911 Acquisition of a number of first-rate works by 14th- and 15th-century artists from Count Grigory Stroganov's collection including the right wing (*Madonna*) of the *Annunciation* diptych by Simone Martini and a reliquary painted by Fra Beato Angelico da Fiesole

1911–15 The Small Hermitage was equipped with heating and ventilation systems

1914 Acquisition of Leonardo da Vinci's *Benois Madonna*

1915 Purchase of Pyotr Semionov-Tianshansky's collection of Dutch and Flemish paintings. Opening of a hospital for wounded soldiers in the Neva and Main Suites of state rooms in the Winter Palace

The Hermitage. History of the Buildings and Collections

The complex of buildings created by talented architects in the very centre of the Russian capital for over a century — since the middle of the 18th century onward — as the state residence of the Russian emperors serves now as a precious setting for the artistic treasures preserved in the State Hermitage which ranks among the best museums in the world. The Winter Palace, the buildings of the Small, Old and New Hermitages and the Hermitage Theatre, located close to the palace, are used now to display the main permanent exhibitions of the museum. In the 1970s the palace of Prince Alexander Menshikov, first governor of St Petersburg, lying on the opposite bank of the Neva (Vasilyevsky Island), became part of the Hermitage. In the 1990s the museum was also given the eastern wing of the former General Staff building that had once housed the Ministries of Foreign Affairs and Finance of the Russian Empire. Not long time ago the Hermitage received two more exhibition spaces — the Museum of Porcelain at the famous Imperial (later Lomonosov) Porcelain Factory and a few rooms in the new Restoration and Storage Centre built in Staraya Derevnya on the outskirts of St Petersburg and equipped to meet the up-to-date museum standards.

Benjamin Paterssen. *Palace Square Viewed from the Beginning of Nevsky Prospekt*. 1800

◀ Konstantin Ukhtomsky. *The Main Staircase*. 1860s

The Winter Palace of Peter I. After the original drawing by Mikhail Makhayev. 1750s

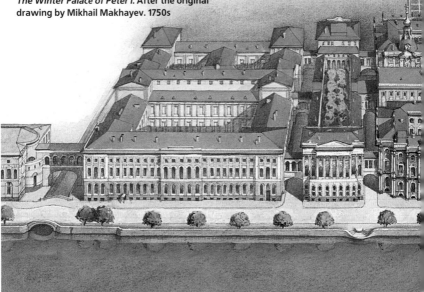

Adolphe Ladurner. *The Ceremonial Consecration of the Alexander Column. 30 August 1834.* 1830s

The Hermitage is generally acknowledged to be one of the richest "encyclopaedic" museums of the world. Its collection outnumbers 3, 000, 000 items, including over 16, 000 paintings, 12, 000 sculptures, almost 300, 000 works of applied art, more than 1, 000, 000 coins, medals and order badges as well as a great amount of arms, banners, books, scientific devices and mechanisms. The entire world culture from the Paleolithic period till modern day seems to be set alive within the museum walls. Unique items, from the artifacts of early civilizations to modern art from the East and West, covering all the types of human creative activities, coexist in harmony in the magnificent palace interiors which themselves represent various styles of Russian architecture and different periods of the country's history.

Catherine II is considered the founder of the museum. The date of its foundation is 1764; in that year the Berlin merchant Johann Ernest Gotzkowski who owed a large sum of money to the Russian Treasury offered to the empress, in payment of his debt, a collection of 225 paintings, mainly works by 17th-century Dutch and Flemish artists. They were exhibited in the Small Hermitage (the word "hermitage" is translated from the French as "a retired place" or "an abode of a recluse") built next to the Winter Palace and intended for private receptions and pastime in the circle of choice guests, which gave its name to the museum. The royal hostess and her guests could get to the Small Hermitage by the specially built passages that linked the two buildings and turned them into a single complex. Later three more palaces were put up next to them and all the five structures formed the famous Hermitage ensemble.

The Gotzkowski collection was followed by numerous new acquisitions. Extensive collections and separate masterpieces were bought at all major European auctions and workshops of leading artists on behalf of the Russian empress. Catherine II did not spare money for this and gained the fame of one of most generous collectors in Europe. Foreign travellers who visited the Hermitage described the palaces and art treasures of the "Russian Semiramis" with admiration and their stories encouraged art dealers to make new most tempting offers. Thus, by the end of the 18th century the picture gallery of Catherine the Great could rival the best collections of Europe, both in the quantity and quality of its art works. Along with paintings, it contained sculptures, engravings, drawings, tapestries, cameos, ivories, faience, glass, bronzes and silver objects, pieces of jewellery made of gold and precious stones. It was in the reign of Catherine II that the first classification of the collection began and in fact two departments of the museum — of the History of European Art and of Numismatics (Munzkabinett) — were formed.

The death of Catherine the Great marked the end of the first, most active period in the formation of the collection. A new stage in the process of developing the private collection into a public museum be-

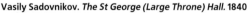

Vasily Sadovnikov. *The St George (Large Throne) Hall.* **1840**

Vasily Sadovnikov. *The Field Marshals Room.* 1840

gan in 1805 when Alexander I issued a decree on the Hermitage. In accordance with this decree all the exhibits were assigned to five departments (the main one being the Picture Gallery). The New Hermitage, first public art museum in Russia, was built by the order of Nicholas I and opened for the public in 1852. The rooms of its second floor housed a major part of the Picture Gallery which comprised paintings by the Flemish, Dutch and Spanish schools and Italian art from the 17th – 18th centuries. The rooms of the first floor were specially designed for displaying Ancient Greek and Roman and European sculptures.

In the early years of the museum's existence its collections were accessible only to the members of high society. The admittance hours were limited; visitors were accompanied by a museum servant and should have a ticket issued by the court office of His Majesty. The men must wear full uniforms and swords and the women must be in the court attire. Visitors were not admitted from half past twelve till quarter past two pm, as "His Majesty Himself used to visit the Hermitage daily at

that time." Nicholas I wanted to direct the work of the museum himself, yet his Instruction on the Maintenance of the Imperial Hermitage, issued twice – in 1851 and 1852, granted the museum status of an independent institution, which was finally confirmed in the 1860s, in the reign of Emperor Alexander II.

At the beginning of the 20th century the Hermitage became the largest scientific museum centre in Europe. However, the beginning of World War I that broke out in 1914 had a great impact on the activities of the museum. St Petersburg, then the capital of Russia, was in a dangerous proximi-

Vasily Sadovnikov. *The 1812 War Gallery in the Winter Palace.* 1840

Edward Hau. *The Pavilion Hall.* 1864

ty to the front and therefore it was decided to take some part of the collection to Moscow. Soon after the October Revolution and the establishment of Soviet power, the newly organized in 1918 Council of the Hermitage took energetic measures to return the evacuated treasures. Nevertheless the display rooms were opened for visitors only on 2 January 1923.

In the 1920s numerous works from nationalized private collections began to arrive in the Hermitage. This period, however, was associated not only with sizeable additions to the collection but with dramatic losses too. In the 1920s – 1930s many of the Hermitage's best art works were sold to foreign countries. The Iron Curtain that separated the USSR and the West destroyed the Hermitage's international scientific, business and even friendly relations. It was due to the activities of Iosif Orbeli who became Hermitage Director in 1934 that the museum retained its position as international cultural space.

The structure of the Hermitage was mainly formed by 1941. Separate collections of Ancient Greek and Roman art that had entered the museum in different periods since the middle of the 18th till the 20th centuries were put together and displayed in the rooms of the New Hermitage. In 1920 the Oriental Department was set up to hold works from this enormous region, works dating from the times of ancient Egypt and Mesopotamia to the 20th century that had been collected for two centuries. 1925 marked the beginning of education activities and introduction of the Education Department. The Department of the History of Primitive Culture (nowadays, the Department of the Archaeology of Eastern Europe and Siberia)

Luigi Primazzi. *The Room of Ancient Sculpture.* 1856

was set up in 1931 for holding and studying antiquities discovered on the territory of Russia. Finally, in 1941, shortly before the beginning of World War II, there was formed the last department – Department of Russian Culture.

During the war the Hermitage staff had managed to send the most valuable part of the museum collections to Sverdlovsk (Yekaterinburg) in the Urals before the Germans closed the circle of siege around the city.

In spite of all the sufferings of the wartime the museum survived and its buildings were not severely damaged. Almost immediately after the lifting of the siege, in January 1944, the Hermitage began to get alive. In the beginning of 1946 Leningraders and guests of the city saw again the famous art works displayed in the same rooms which had been completely restored and opened to the public.

Two years later an important event took place – the museum received 298 canvases by the French Impressionists and Post-Impressionists, such as Henri Matisse, Pablo Picasso and other artists of the early 20th century, as well as several first-rate canvases by Wassily Kandinsky that came from the Museum of New Western Art in Moscow shut down before the war. Thus the foundation of the collection of modern European art was laid. Its bulk was made up by the famous collections of the two well-known Moscow art patrons, Sergei Shchukin and Ivan Morozov. Two directors of the Hermitage Mikhail Artamonov and Boris Piotrovsky, talented scholars devoted to the museum, greatly contributed to its development in the second half of the 20th century. The latter was in charge of the Hermitage for almost a quarter of the century – from 1964 till 1990.

Important changes took place in the Hermitage, as well as in the whole of the country, in the difficult 1990s, when it was headed by Mikhail Piotrovsky. The muse-

Konstantin Ukhtomsky.
The Malachite Room. **1865**

um, considered traditional and highly conservative, turned into a rapidly developing modern international multifunctional cultural and scientific institution that has its branches in different cities of Russia and abroad, opened in accordance with the "Greater Hermitage" project.

The beginning of the complete restoration of the General Staff building, which had been waited for so long and which is to be finished by 2014 to mark the 250th anniversary of the museum, became another vital event in the Hermitage history. The great museum goes on living and developing...

Edward Hau. *The Small Church.* **1862**

The Winter Palace

History and Architecture

The Palace Bridge across the Neva, which links the central part of the city to Vasilyevsky Island, affords a breathtaking view of Palace Square with a panorama of the Hermitage complex. Its most prominent landmark is the Winter Palace built in 1754–62 to a design by Francesco Bartolomeo Rastrelli (1700–1771). The great architect was the son of Bartolomeo Carlo Rastrelli (1675–1744), an Italian sculptor invited to Russia by Peter the Great. The newly established capital of Russia was in that period the most suitable place for implementing the most daring architectural fantasies. Architects had at their disposal vast open spaces which seemed to be intended for majestic large-scale ensembles. The flowering of Rastrelli's genius coincided with the reign of Elizabeth Petrovna, daughter of Peter the Great, who ascended the throne in November 1741 in the result of a palace coup led by the Guards. The first Winter Palace had been put up in St Petersburg earlier, during the reign of Peter the Great. The site on the bank of the Neva, chosen by the founder of the Northern capital, was not moved far during the construction of the later Winter Palaces – the buildings just shifted little by little towards the Admiralty; their dimensions grew and their architectural design became more and more rich and elaborate.

Pietro Rotari. *Portrait of the Architect Francesco Bartolomeo Rastrelli*

◀ **View of the Winter Palace from the River Neva**

For six years the best masons brought to St Petersburg from different cities of Russia had been building in the centre of the city the palace that would become one of the most elegant royal residences in Europe. At last, in the spring of 1761, the new majestic edifice was completed. It proved to be a fine example of the Russian Baroque and Rastrelli's most perfect creation. Long work on the decoration of the numerous interiors began. Seemingly foreseeing her forthcoming demise, the empress pressed the architect to complete the decora-

Main (Jordan) Staircase

tion of the rooms and halls as quick as possible. Elizabeth Petrovna, however, did not live to move into the newly built residence – she died on 25 December 1761.

It was a new Empress Catherine II, who had received the title in the result of another palace coup in June 1762, who moved into the palace. This event marked the beginning of the history of the official Imperial residence inseparably connected with the formation of the Hermitage Museum collections.

The Main (Jordan) Staircase

Passing under the austere white-marble arches of the first-floor gallery we find ourselves on the huge space of the Main Staircase which has two flights of stairs. The brilliant architect of the 18th century, Francesco Bartolomeo Rastrelli, was at his very best in this interior. The sunlight flooding from the windows and reflected in the mirrors of the opposite wall streams along the gilded moulded ornaments and the white marble of the statues of deities and the Muses adorning this sumptuous interior, making it even more impressive. Located almost at the height of twenty metres, the ceiling painting that features ancient gods hovering in the sky enhances the illusory effect of infinite space in the Baroque manner. It is hard to believe that in the 18th century the interior used to have another plafond later destroyed by fire. The present-day ceiling painting by the Italian decorator Gasparo Damiani had once adorned a hall in the palace. The architect Vasily Stasov discovered it in a storeroom during restoration work and although the canvas was a little smaller than the original one, the architect perfectly fitted it into Rastrelli's composition. The subject of the painting, in combination with the sculptural allegories of Loyalty, Justice, Grandeur, Wisdom, Equity and Opulence set in the niches, emphasized the significance of the principal Imperial residence as a dwelling of earthly gods, an abode of virtues.

The Field Marshals Room

The Field Marshals Room, designed in 1833–34 by Auguste de Montferrand and restored after the fire by Vasily Stasov, is embellished with portraits of most prominent Russian military figures and serves as a sort of prelude to the majestic architectural "oratory" created by the great architect. This austere white-marble room has an ill repute – it was here that the conflagration, which destroyed the entire Winter Palace, began on 17 December 1837. The doors of the Field Marshals Room lead onto the next interiors of the two main state suites and other rooms of the Winter Palace.

The Peter I (Small Throne) Room

The Peter I (or Small Throne) Room is devoted to the memory of Peter the Great, the founder of the Russian Empire. The room was designed by Auguste de Montferrand in 1833 and restored after fire by Vasily Stasov almost without any alterations. All the details of the architectural decor are connected with the name of the great Russian reformer. In the centre of the hall, in a semicircular niche, is an allegorical canvas, *Peter the Great with the Goddess of Wisdom Minerva* by Jacopo Amigoni. Near it, on a special dais, stands the tsar's throne made by the German master Christian Meyer for Emperor Paul I (it is a copy of the throne in the Large Throne Room commissioned by Empress Anna Ioannovna from the English master craftsman Nicholas Clausen). The walls of the room are lined with red Lyons velvet embroidered with a silver ornament. Interwoven into the ornament are the repeatedly used elements of the Imperial attributes: the monogramme of Peter the Great, the tsar's crown and the state emblem in the shape of double-headed eagle. Imperial symbolism included into the ornamental design of the ceiling and the painted

Field Marshals Room

The grand building of the palace, occupying a huge area, with a large inner courtyard and small patios open to the sky in its corner parts, had a majestic look from the Neva embankment, the Admiralty and Palace Square overlooked by its main facade with a monumental triple arcade. The dynamic silhouettes of the walls, the virtuoso delineation of the Baroque ornaments and the abundance of moulded decor never ceased to evoke admiration of the contemporaries. The colouring of the walls at first imitated natural stone thus lending the palace a great elegance – the walls were painted in "sand colour with a slight tinge of yellow and ornaments were executed in white lime." The decoration of the interiors impressed the visitors by its luxury and a variety of forms.

Peter I (Small Throne) Room

The facades of Rastrelli's outstanding creation have basically retained their original appearance to this day. Only the pieces of sculpture decorating the roof were replaced in the late 19th century, and the colour of the walls and decor was altered several times. As for the palace rooms and halls, they were often redecorated. Every new Imperial family refurnished their living apartments to meet the day's fashions and their own tastes and needs, changing their planning, structure and decor. The best architects active in Russia – Yury Velten, Jean-Baptiste Vallin de la Mothe, Antonio Rinaldi, Giacomo Quarenghi, Ivan Starov, Carlo Rossi and Auguste de Montferrand – took part in the planning and design of the interiors. An important landmark in the history of the royal palace was a great fire that broke out on 17–19 December 1837 and practically erased its interiors. The restoration of the palace was carried out in 1837–39 under the supervision of Vasily Stasov (1769–1848) and Alexander Briullov (1798–1877).

The present-day Winter Palace is a fanciful combination of various styles and ages as well as architectural fantasies by famous architects blending, however, into a single magnificent whole. Nowadays, only a few original interiors of the Winter Palace give an idea of the gran-

decorative panels featuring the famous battles of the Northern War – the Battle of Poltava and the Battle of Lesnaya – promoted the perception of this interior as the "palladium of Russian grandeur and glory."

The Armorial Hall

Each of the subsequent rooms of the suite develops the theme of the celebration of the Fatherland's military glory. The Armorial Hall created by Vasily Stasov vividly contrasts with the adjacent Peter I Room not only by its scale, but also by its bright colour scheme, unusually vivid for Classicism. This exemplar of a Classical columned hall belonged to the formal reception rooms of the Winter Palace and served as an introductory interior to the St George Hall. Intended for the receptions of the Russian nobility, representatives of different Russian provinces, the hall must have been very impressive in its look. The stately image of the Armorial Hall is emphasized by the majestic rhythm of its French windows alternating with the massive columns gilded from top to bottom (according to the

Armorial Hall

original design of Stasov only their grooves were to be gilded). They are vividly reflected in the mirrored windows of the opposite wall. The main theme of the suite is boldly expressed in the decor: near the side walls are placed sculptural groups of ancient Russian knights holding standards to which coloured signs with emblems of the Russian provinces were attached. The same heraldic motif was included into the decor of huge bronze chandeliers. They are adorned with the coats-of-arms of Russian cities to this day.

The 1812 War Gallery

It is the most famous memorial room of the palace dedicated to the victory of the Russian Army. Lying between the two main formal interiors – the Armorial Hall and the St George Hall – it was designed by Carlo Rossi and the ceremony of its opening was held on 25 December 1826, the anniversary of Napoleon's expulsion from Russia. 332 portraits of participants in the War of 1812 are hung on its walls – the war generals or those who received a general's rank right after the end of the war. Thirteen places for portraits are left empty, likenesses of these generals perished in the war were not found. All the portraits were painted in the studio of George Dawe, an English painter invited by Alexander I to carry out this large commission in Russia. The gallery also housed large-scale formal portraits of the European monarchs, the allies of Russia in the anti-Napoleonic coalition, and portraits of military leaders. Moreover, for the first time in the history of the Imperial residence the gallery was adorned with portraits of rankers from the Company of the Palace Grenadiers who rescued all the canvases during the

1812 War Gallery

deur and scope of Rastrelli's genius, his grandiose Baroque designs. One of them is a majestic Main (Jordan) Staircase. Together with the most representative official part of the palace it leads into, the staircase was destroyed by fire in 1837. Vasily Stasov, who supervised the restoration of the destroyed interiors and redesigned many of them, succeeded in re-creating the original look of the staircase and retaining Rastrelli's main concept.

The Jordan Staircase affords a view of two state suites of the palace – the Main Suite and the Neva Suite overlooking the Neva embankment. The former was a complex of interiors used for official ceremonies. The rooms were almost completely destroyed by fire and Stasov restored them to their original grandeur and magnificence. The splendid decor of the Field Marshals, Peter I (Small Throne) Rooms, Armorial Hall, 1812 War Gallery and St George Hall were designed to celebrate the outstanding events of Russian history and their participants.

St George (Large Throne) Hall

In Rastrelli's palace the enfilade of rooms running from the Main Staircase alongside the Neva ended with the Throne Room striking by its Baroque opulence. In the late 18th century Giacomo Quarenghi, court architect to Catherine the Great, moved the main state hall of the royal residence to a specially built wing on the side of the Great Courtyard. Instead of the five rooms of the Neva Suite he created three new interiors – the Anteroom, the Large Anteroom, or Nicholas Hall, and the Concert Hall. The decor of these formal halls, where the cream of the Russian aristocracy, foreign ambassadors and celebrated guests of the Imperial family used to gather for balls, performances and concerts, was markedly altered. The unbridled Baroque fantasies were ousted by the elegant restraint of Classicism based on a subtle chromatic play of various artificial marbles facing the walls and columns.

The architect Vasily Stasov, who restored the Neva Suite after the fire of 1837, kept Quarenghi's design largely unaltered. However, he made the halls even more imposing and monumental – the white marble of the walls and columns further enhanced the immense space of the halls

fire of 1837 (the portraits were returned to the their original places after Stasov's restoration of the interior). Later the portrait of Alexander I by Dawe was replaced by another one painted by Franz von Kruger.

The St George Hall

The 1812 War Gallery opens up the space of the St George (Large Throne) Hall, an architectural and thematic culmination of the Main Suite, which was ceremoniously opened on 26 November (9 December – New Style) 1795 on the feast day of St George. Catherine the Great commissioned the architect Giacomo Quarenghi to design a new throne room instead of Rastrelli's outfashioned Baroque hall which no longer satisfied the rational spirit of the Enlightenment. Created in 1787–1795, the interior was resolved in austere Classical forms. Quarenghi's recognized masterpiece was a splendid monumental hall with two tiers of windows adorned with double columns of natural coloured marble. When Vasily Stasov restored it after the fire he preserved only the general proportions and architectural articulations of the interior. Emperor Nicholas I ordered to make "the entire St George Hall in white marble." The walls and columns were faced by expensive white Carrara marble with bluish streaks which was brought in the form of slabs and even whole columns from Italy. The favourite material of Italian sculptors sparkling with thousands of shades, enhanced the varicoloured palette of the inlaid parquet floor made up of sixteen different kinds of wood. The ornament of the floor repeated in the mirror-like manner in the golden pattern embossed in the copper of the suspended metal ceiling. The marble bas-relief with a representation of the victorious St George by the Italian master Francesco del Nero was placed above the throne. The St George Hall was consecrated later than other rooms in the palace – in 1841 – owing to the difficulties related to the delivery from Italy and the mounting of fragile marble details. The Large Throne Hall, one of the best formal interiors designed by Stasov, befittingly completes the Main Suite of the Winter Palace. It was here and in the next Grand Church that the formal royal "grand entrees," started in the private quarters and held strictly according to the rules, ended.

Cupola of the Grand Church

The Grand Church

The Grand Church, which received the status of cathedral in 1807, had been designed in the cause of the construction of the Winter Palace by Francesco Bartolomeo Rastrelli and consecrated in honour of the Resurrection of Christ in 1762. A year later an *Image of Our Lord-Not-Made-by-Hands* was

Grand Church

reflected in the mirrors and filling it with air. The elements of decor began to look larger and even more ceremonious. Today temporary exhibitions are mounted in the well-lit Neva Suite of rooms and halls.

The living quarters of the Imperial family from the late 18th – early 20th centuries have not preserved their original look. A few extant watercolours and drawings represent the Winter Palace interiors, later destroyed by fire or changed to match the fashion of the day, as they once used to be.

After the fire Alexander Briullov was in charge of the restoration of this part of the palace. In 1838–39 he continued Stasov's tradition of expressing the themes of the Russian Empire's grandeur and glory in architectural forms. Thus he designed the Alexander Hall in the southern part of the Winter Palace commemorating Emperor Alexander I and next five rooms that contained military paintings recording the Russian Army's victories. The windows of the rooms overlooked Palace Square, in the centre of which stood the ceremonious Alexander Column that echoed the memorial ensemble of the palace interiors. One of the owners of the living quarters located in this part was the first hostess of the Winter Palace Catherine II; her apartments were to be found next to the Grand Church.

transferred here and the church was rededicated to the icon. When Stasov was restoring the interior, he was set the task of recreating its original look. He aimed not only at restoring its Baroque decoration but also at recreating Rastrelli's original composition. He opened up the cupola covered before the fire, thus returning to the church one of its main features and its most important symbol of an Orthodox Church. In 1838–39 Fyodor Bruni and Pyotr Basin restored the monumental paintings by the Italian artist Francesco Fontebasso lost in the fire – figures of the Evangelists on the vaults and the *Resurrection of Christ* composition on the flat ceiling of the anteroom. Most of the decorative elements are made of papier-mache, the material first used by Stasov in the Tsarskoye Selo palace church in 1820. As the time allotted for the restoration of the Winter Palace was very short, papier-mache decoration was a good substitute for time-consuming wood carving. The latter technique was employed only for the most important element of the church – its magnificent iconostasis made by P. Cretan and dismantled in the 1940s.

The Nicholas (Large) Hall

It is the largest state room of the Winter Palace (its area is 1,103 m^2) and the focal point of the Neva Suite. In Quarenghi's time it was known as the Large Anteroom, but in 1856, when a large portrait of Nicholas I by Franz von Kruger was installed here, it was named after the deceased emperor.

The Concert Hall

It adjoins the Nicholas (Large) Hall. It was used for concerts

Nicholas Hall (Large Anteroom)

Concert Hall

and theatrical performances. Its purpose could be easily guessed from its decor – its second tier has statues of the Muses and classical deities by the sculptor Johann Hermann, while the grisaille painting of the cove linking the ceiling and the walls includes allegorical figures with attributes of the arts.

The Concert Hall displays of the Hermitage collection of Russian silverware from the 17th to the early 20th centuries, a unique 18th-century memorial complex, the silver shrine of St Alexander Nevsky, which is the centrepiece.

This unusual monument to the famous Russian statesman and military leader of the 13th century, canonized by the Russian Ortodox Chirch, was commissioned by Empress Elizabeth Petrovna. It was made of 90 poods of silver – an annual output of silver in the Kolyvan mines (Altai).

The rooms facing the Admiralty and occupied by Tsesarevich Alexander Nikolayevich were of special historical interest. They had been originally designed by the architect Giacomo Quarenghi as early as 1791 for the grandson of Catherine II, Grand Duke Alexander I. After his coronation, however, Emperor Alexander I moved to another part of the palace leaving these quarters first to his brother Constantine and later to another brother Nicholas. When Nicholas Pavlovich ascended the throne, he kept the tradition and gave these apartments to his son. Due to the great historical significance of these apartments, where three Russian monarchs had spent their childhood, their decoration was never altered in the cause of repairs. Even after the fire Briullov reproduced the style of Quarenghi "in minutest detail."

White Room

Most characteristic example of Briullov's style is an ensemble of interiors created for the wedding of the Heir Apparent, future Emperor Alexander II. Work on it started simultaneously with the restoration of the Winter Palace after the fire and was completed in April 1841. The so-called New Apartments of the Heir Apparent actually became the quarters of Alexander II's spouse, Maria Alexandrovna, nee Maximiliana-Wilhelmina, Duchess of Hessen-Darmstadt. The decoration of the White Room and Golden Dwelling Room as well as of her private living quarters including the Crimson Study,

Golden Dwelling Room

The White Room

It is the main formal room of the so-called New Apartments of the Heir Apparent. This large room lit by two tiers of windows seems to be over-decorated with moulded ornaments and statues, yet Alexander Briullov created the interior proportions to counterbalance its volume and abundance of the decorative elements.

The Golden Dwelling Room

Neighbouring the White Room in the so-called New Apartments of the Heir Apparent, it was designed by Alexander Briullov to contrast the former in its size and decoration. The room embodies the ideas of eclecticism or historicism, based on the free choice of architectural sources when the architect combines absolutely different plastic forms and historic impressions and gives free rein to his fantasies. In accordance with Briullov's idea, its decoration was to echo that of the main dwelling room of Empress Alexandra Fyodorovna, wife of Nicholas I, which was known as the Golden Dwelling Room (now Malachite Room). Originally the walls and vault of the Golden Dwelling Room were covered with white artificial marble and gilding was used only to highlight the thin moulded ornament. The furniture, however, was completely gilded. The shining of the gilded elements was emphasized by the panels fashioned of lapis lazuli, a blue semi-precious stone. Other elements of the decor included a superb marble fireplace with a mosaic composition, jasper columns and gilded doors with carved ornaments. In the 1860s and 1870s the walls of the hall were gilded all over.

The Boudoir

It is one of the most exquisite interiors of the Winter Palace. Originally designed by Alexander Bruillov as one of the private rooms of the so-called New Apartments of the Heir Apparent, it was completely reshaped in 1853 by Harald Bosse (1812–1894), in keeping with the demands of a new fashion. Like an elegant snuff-box, this small room is stylized in the spirit of Rococo with an abundance of carved and gilded ornaments, mirrors and painted insets. A part of the Boudoir, shaped like an alcove, is separated by a step and a low railing. At first the architect wanted to emphasize this separation by colour and to line the walls of the alcove in white textile, while the rest of the Boudoir was crimson. Later Bruillov gave up the idea and designed the entire room in the same colour scale. The cloth of pomegranate shade for the wall panels, furniture upholstery, draperies on the windows and doors was commissioned in

Blue Bedroom, Bathroom, Toilette Room and Green Dining Room has survived to our day.

One of the most famous and lavish interiors designed by Briullov in the Winter Palace is the Malachite Room, which was part of the suite of the private apartments of Nicholas I's wife, Empress Alexandra Fyodorovna, nee princess Charlotte of Prussia. In tune with Nicholas's wish, Briullov used precious malachite from the Urals for the decoration of this room.

Adjoining the living quarters of Nicholas I's family was the elegant circular Rotunda created in the 1830s by Auguste de Montferrand and also restored by Briullov.

Boudoir

In the mid-1890s some of the living quarters were significantly changed. In 1894 the architect Alexander Krasovsky, who had previously been an engineer on the staff of the Court Office, began to redecorate a set of apartments for the future Russian Emperor Nicholas II. After Nicholas Alexandrovich's ascension to the throne on 30 December 1895, his family moved to live in the Winter Palace. A set of rooms following the Malachite Room was turned into the living quarters of his wife Empress Alexandra Fyodorovna. Their once sumptuous decoration designed by Briullov was replaced by a simpler one which made the rooms cosier and more suitable for private life. The apartments

Malachite Room

of Nicholas II, to which the Saltykov Staircase led from the Admiralty side, were also marked not so much by luxury but rather by comfort and cosiness. Set next to the bed chambers, dwelling and dining rooms were smoking and billiard rooms, libraries, bathrooms and children playrooms.

A noteworthy detail in one of the rooms in the former living quarters of the last Imperial family (Small Dining Room) reminds of a drastic change in the history of the country. The hands of the massive mantle clock show 10 minutes past two. It was at that night hour that members of the Provisional Government were arrested in the Small Dining Room on 7 November (25 October Old Style) 1917. A new era of Russian history began.

France at the Cortier Factory. For the overdoor decorations Bosse used paintings from the Hermitage stocks.

The Malachite Room (Malachite Dwelling Room)

The Urals malachite, strikingly beautiful and rare green stone, was used since the 18th century for the facing of table decorations, snuff-boxes, ink sets and vases. It began to be more widely employed for interior decor in the 1830s, after huge deposits of malachite had been discovered at the Demidovs' mines in the Urals. Malachite was used in the drawing room of Empress Alexandra Fyodorovna to face the columns, pilasters and fireplace, by means of the complex and laborious technique known as "Russian mosaic." Thin layers of malachite were pasted onto the base and the joints were filled with malachite powder, then the surface was polished.

The combination of malachite with rich gilding of the vault, doors, capitals of the columns and pilasters produced a striking effect. Guests did not know what to amaze more at — the luxury of the material or the luxury of the artist's work — in this temple of wealth and taste. The southern wall faced with white marble was embellished with the allegorical representations of Day, Night and Poetry done by A. Vighi. The room was set with furniture executed in the 1830s by the cabinet-maker Heinrich Gambs after drawings by Auguste de Montferrand and saved during the fire. The heavy sofas, armchairs and tables produced an impression that the "furniture was forged of gold" and this effect perfectly matched the overall style of the room. The crimson upholstery seemed to be another vivid accent in the effective combination of red, green and golden.

The Library

This stunning well-preserved room used to be part of the living quarters of Nicholas II. Its decor with the heavy carved walnut ceiling, marble fireplaces and bookcases abundantly embellished with carved ornaments is designed to imitate the Gothic style.

The Small Dining Room

The Small Dining Room is another room in the living quarters of the last Imperial family that has preserved its decor from the late 19th century. This small room set next to the Malachite Room and designed in the Rococo style was used for private family dinners. The walls are hung with tapestries made at the St Petersburg Tapestry Factory for the "Parts of the World" series.

Library

Small Dining Room

French Art: 15th – 18th Centuries

SECOND FLOOR: ROOMS 272–297

The rooms of the Winter Palace that once served as living and auxiliary quarters house collections of various Hermitage departments today. Displayed on the three floors of the museum are their exhibits that cover a long period from Primitive culture to modern day and include archaeological artifacts, objects fashioned by Oriental craftsmen, works by European and Russian artists.

The Hermitage's famous collection of French art from the 15th – 20th centuries fills more than fifty rooms and represents a wide panorama of practically all the styles and trends as well as best-known painters, sculptors and masters of applied art. There is no collection outside France capable to rival the Hermitage in the quantity and quality of superb examples of the French school. Many of the masterpieces dating from the 16th – 18th centuries were acquired by Catherine the Great, known as an ardent admirer of French style and fashion.

The flowering of the Renaissance in France that began in the 16th century is represented by Bernard Palissy's faience, Limoges enamels, furniture and tapestries. The small, yet excellent Hermitage collection of French portraiture enables us to form a good notion of refined French Renaissance culture which combined aristocratic purity of style with a love for characteristic individual features. In the 17th century the "golden age" of French culture started its triumph all over Europe. The art of this period is well represented in the Hermitage collection by works of Nicolas Poussin and Louis Le Nain. The notion of the applied art from the reign of Louis XIV is given by Andre-Charles Boulle's pieces exhibited in the Hermitage. Magnificent porcelain sets produced by the Sevres Factory, a great number of tapestries, exquisite furniture, silver and bronze decorations lend a festive look to the rooms displaying canvases by 18th-century artists: Antoine Watteau, Francois Boucher, Jean-Honore Fragonard and others. The Hermitage possesses one of the best collections of 18th-century French easel sculpture which includes several works by Etienne-Maurice Falconet.

MASTER OF THE THUISON ALTARPIECE

The Entry into Jerusalem. Second half of the 15th century. Oil on panel. 116.5 x 51.5 cm

This artist, who was active in Amiens, received his name after his only known work, an altarpiece from the city of Thuison. The Hermitage piece is one of the eight panels from the altar screen (other seven panels are held in the Art Institute of Chicago). Works by French painters from the 15th century are extremely rare outside France. This makes even more valuable the Hermitage's bright-coloured wing of the altarpiece, the *Entry into Jerusalem*, painted with an almost Netherlandish loving attention to detail. Interest in the real world is combined here with the exquisite manner of painting highly characteristic of French art.

JACQUES BELLANGE

Active in 1602–17

Only a few works by Jacques Bellange, who was born in Lotharingia (Lorraine) and most probably was the court painter, engraver and decorator to the Dukes of Lorraine, have survived. The fact lends even more importance to the *Lamentation* which has relatively recently entered the Hermitage. It comes from a private collection where it was ascribed to Caravaggio. In the cause of restoration, however, it has been reattributed first to the French school in general and later to Bellange in particular.

Jacques Bellange. *The Lamentation.* 1615–17. Oil on canvas. 115 x 175 cm

Corneille de Lyon. *Portrait of a Woman.*
Mid-1530s. Oil on panel. 20 x 15.5 cm

CORNEILLE DE LYON
Early 16th century – 1575

Corneille de Lyon was a prominent Renaissance portrait painter who mostly worked on commissions from the royal family. The model for the portrait must have been some lady of the court of Francis I whose reign was marked by the culmination of the French Renaissance.

JEAN GOUJON
1510–1568

The only specimen of Renaissance sculpture in the Hermitage collection – the marble relief *Venus and Cupid* – is attributed to the celebrated French sculptor Jean Goujon, who was close to the Fontainebleau school.

Jean Goujon (?). *Venus and Cupid.* Marble. 51 x 57 cm

SIMON VOUET
1590–1649

Simon Vouet, the court painter to Louis XIII, expressed all the peculiar traits of the "grand style" in his typical formal painting – the *Allegorical Portrait of Queen Anne of Austria* which shows her as goddess of wisdom Minerva.

Simon Vouet. *Allegorical Portrait of Queen Anne of Austria as Minerva.* Circa 1643. Oil on canvas. 202 x 172 cm

Louis Le Nain. *Milkmaid's Family.* 1640s.
Oil on canvas. 51 x 59 cm

LOUIS LE NAIN
1593–1648

The Hermitage has two paintings by Louis Le Nain – the world-famous *Milkmaid's Family* and an earlier canvas, *A Visit to Grandmother*. The subject of *Milkmaid's Family*, a painting classed with the so-called "peasant genre," is, however, devoid of any everyday narrative details or entertaining features. The figures of French peasants, shown immobile against the background of the immense, grey-bluish sky – are full of epic grandeur, like classicist personages of Nicolas Poussin.

Nicolas Poussin. *Tancred and Erminia.* Mid-1630s. Oil on canvas. 98.5 x 146.4 cm

Nicolas Poussin. *Venus, Faun and Putti.*
1630s. Oil on canvas. 72 x 56 cm

NICOLAS POUSSIN
1594–1665

Nicolas Poussin, founder of the French Classicism, is represented in the Hermitage by twelve paintings revealing the essence of his painterly system. The blend of reasonable clarity of the composition and profound lyrical feeling distinguishes the painting *Tancred and Erminia*, a masterpiece in the Poussin collection. The picture is based on a subject borrowed from *Jerusalem Delivered*, a great poem by the Italian Renaissance author Torquato Tasso. In the late 1640s

Nicolas Poussin. *Landscape with Polythemus.* 1649. Oil on canvas. 150 x 199 cm

Poussin created a series of majestic and beautiful landscapes devoted to the harmonious unity of eternal Nature and all creatures inhabiting it. The earth, trees, mountains, gods, people, nymphs and satyrs in the *Landscape with Polythemus* seem to listen, holding their breath, to the magic sounds of the pipe played by the Cyclops Polythemus who suffers from his unrequited love to the nymph Galatea.

FRANCOIS GIRARDON
1628–1715

Francois Girardon was a leading sculptor in the 17th century. His monument to Louis XIV was erected in 1699 on the Place Vendome in Paris, but destroyed during the French Revolution. Its model held in the Hermitage helps the viewer gain the idea of the appearance of the monument. In tune with the academic tradition, equestrian statues were to reproduce original Ancient Roman works. The prototype for Girardon's composition was the statue of Marcus Aurelius on the Capitoline Hill.

Francois Girardon. Model for the equestrian statue of Louis XIV. 1692. Bronze. Height 108 cm

Claude Lorrain (Claude Gellee). *Morning in the Harbour.* 1640s. Oil on canvas. 74 x 97 cm

CLAUDE LORRAIN (CLAUDE GELLEE)
1600–1682

Claude Lorrain developed in his landscapes the elevated Classical 17th-century style introduced by Poussin. His works, including twelve Hermitage pieces, are created by the imagination of the artist who strives to express the perfection of nature in pictorial terms. Still his views of the natural scenery were inspired by the real features of Lorrain's beloved Roman Campania.

Antoine Watteau. *Actors of the Comedie-Francaise.* Circa 1712. Oil on panel. 20 x 25 cm

ANTOINE WATTEAU
1684–1721

Antoine Watteau is recognized as a seminal figure of the style that determined the character of French art and culture in the 18th century – the Rococo. He introduced a special kind of festive scenes, so called *fetes galantes*, in which elegant and gracious characters performed, with a tinge of irony, scenes from a spectacle about mysterious and intriguing relations between men and women. Such are his *Embarrassing Proposal* and *Capricious Woman. Savoyard with a Marmot* demonstrates Watteau's interest in subjects borrowed from real life. Savoyards were the inhabitants of the Savoy Mountains known for their extreme poverty who often earned their living by playing the barrel organ.

Antoine Watteau. *Savoyard with a Marmot.* Circa 1716. Oil on canvas. 40.5 x 32.5 cm

Antoine Watteau. *An Embarrassing Proposal.* Circa 1716. Oil on canvas. 65 x 84.5 cm

Antoine Watteau. *The Capricious Woman.* Circa 1718. Oil on canvas. 42 x 34 cm

Nicolas Lancret. *Mlle Camargo Dancing.* 1730s. Oil on canvas. 45 x 55 cm

NICOLAS LANCRET
1690–1743

The pictorial manner and composition of *Mlle Camargo Dancing* betrays the influence of Watteau. Lancret was his pupil and follower. The ballerina of the Paris Opera Ballet who gained fame in the illustrious period of Philippe I, Duc d'Orleans, who served as regent for young King Louis XV, is portrayed at the moment of dancing.

FRANCOIS BOUCHER
1703–1770

The festive and lively spirit of the Rococo is perfectly embodied in the works of Francois Boucher. The most fashionable artist of his time, he had the title of the first painter to the king. The *Toilet of Venus* set into the fashionable oval form and dedicated to the goddess of love demonstrates Boucher as decorator at his best.

Francois Boucher. *The Toilet of Venus.* Oil on canvas. 101 x 86.7 cm

Francois Boucher. *Landscape near Beauvais.* Early 1740s. Oil on canvas. 49 x 58 cm

JEAN-BAPTISTE PERRONNEAU
1715–1783

The favourite medium of Perronneau, brilliant portrait painter, was pastel, yet his *Portrait of a Boy with a Book* done in oil, from the Hermitage collection, is in no way inferior. In his free manner of painting and subtle psychological characteristics he was equal to his better-known compatriots, La Tour, Chardin and Fragonard.

Jean-Baptiste Perronneau. *Portrait of a Boy with a Book.* Mid-1740s. Oil on canvas. 63 x 52 cm

ETIENNE–MAURICE FALCONET
1716–1791

Though Falconet began his artistic career during the refined Rococo age, he imbibed the dramatic expressiveness of the Baroque and assimilated the perfect poise of Classicism. It was not by chance that he was invited by Catherine the Great to St Petersburg for the creation of a monument to Peter the Great (this work became famous as the *Bronze Horseman*).

Threatening Cupid is one of the most popular statues of the Rococo period known in numerous replicas. The graceful figure of the mischievous god of love was commissioned from Falconet by his patroness, Marquise de Pompadour, a favourite of King Louis XV. Many exquisite statuettes in biscuit (unglazed porcelain) were produced after the sketches of Falcone who headed the design studio of the Sevres Porcelain Factory.

Etienne–Maurice Falconet. *Threatening Cupid.* 1758. Marble. Height 85 cm

Jean-Baptiste Simeon Chardin. *Saying Grace before Meal.* 1744.
Oil on canvas. 49.3 x 38.4 cm

Jean-Baptiste Simeon Chardin. *The Washerwoman.* 1730s. Oil on canvas. 37.5 x 42.7 cm

Jean–Baptiste Simeon Chardin. *Still Life with Attributes of the Arts.* 1766.
Oil on canvas. 112 x 140.5 cm

JEAN–BAPTISTE SIMEON CHARDIN
1699–1779

The work of Jean-Baptiste Simeon Chardin developed along the lines of the main ideas of the age of Enlightenment – a brief yet remarkable period in French culture in the second half of the 18th century. His pictures representing the life of the third-estate people prove his ability to discern spiritual essence, harmony and poetics in everyday life.

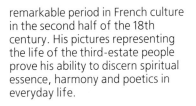

JEAN–ANTOINE HOUDON
1741–1828

The philosophical and aesthetic ideals of the great French Encyclopaedists Voltaire, Diderot, Rousseau and Montesquieu had a great impact on the oeuvre of Jean-Antoine Houdon.
For Houdon Voltaire was the embodiment of the spiritual perfection. The sculptor has done several portraits of the famous philosopher, one of them gracing the foyer of the Comedie-Francaise. The Hermitage statue is its replica commissioned by Catherine II.

Jean–Antoine Houdon.
Voltaire in an Armchair. 1781.
Marble. Height 138 cm

Jean-Baptiste Greuze. *The Paralytic.* 1763. Oil on canvas. 115.5 x 146 cm

JEAN-BAPTISTE GREUZE
1725–1805

Greuze's painting fully manifests the ideas of the Enlightenment. His works praise the virtues of the third-estate people. One of them, the *Paralytic, or Filial Piety* was purchased by Catherine II on advice from Denis Diderot who was much impressed with the artist's work.

JEAN-HONORE FRAGONARD
1732–1806

The brilliant work of Jean-Honore Fragonard was the last outburst of departing Rococo art. The Hermitage has three of his works, one of them being the *Stolen Kiss*. The painting recalls masterpieces by the Small Dutch Masters, yet the sharpness of the scene seemingly spied in a casual manner endows the canvas with a distinctly French charm.

Jean-Honore Fragonard. *The Stolen Kiss.* Late 1780s.
Oil on canvas. 45 x 55 cm

Tapestry: *May. Saint–Germain. The King Riding with the Ladies of the Court.*
"Months, or Royal Households" series
Late 17th – early 18th centuries
Gobelins Tapestry Manufactory, Paris
Wool and silk; tapestry technique.
368 x 303 cm

The Hermitage owns one of the largest collections of French 17th- and 18th-century tapestries. These carpets showing superb many-figured compositions were produced mainly at the Gobelins Royal Manufactory. They were based on sketches by notable painters and woven in wool with an addition of golden and silver thread.

Cabinet. Workshop of Andre-Charles Boulle.
Second half of the 17th century. Paris
Ebony, tortoise-shell and gilded bronze;
marquetry and intarsia. 255 x 170 x 64 cm

The applied art of the "grand style" from the reign of Louis XIV is distinguished by luxury and sumptuousness. The brilliant cabinet-maker from the period, Andre-Charles Boulle, gave his name to the decoration technique he had invented. It was a special fashion of inlaying gilded metal and melted tortoise-shell ornaments onto the ebony base.

British Art: 16th − 19th Centuries
SECOND FLOOR: ROOMS 298−301

The collection of the British school is exhibited next to the displays of 18th-century French art. It is not large, yet its quality provides a comprehensive coverage of the British national tradition and its characteristic features. The majority of the works that can be seen in the Hermitage rooms devoted to British painting are portraits. This reflects the specific character of British art − starting from the period of the establishment of portraiture in the 16th century, it was considered the leading branch of art. England entered the period of the Renaissance rather late, in the second half of the 16th century. In the 18th century British painting came to the period of its flowering associated with the names of three outstanding artists − William Hogarth, Joshua Reynolds and Thomas Gainsborough. Unfortunately, the Hermitage does not possess any works by Hogarth.

In the 18th century many objects of applied art produced in Great Britain, particularly its silverware, faience and gems, were added to the collections of the Russian Imperial family and aristocracy. One of the best-known exhibits is the Green Frog Service made by Wedgwood.

◀ **Room of British Art: 16th − 17th Centuries**

Anonymous artist from the late 16th century. *Portrait of a Man.* (Circle of Marcus Geeraerts the Younger). 1595. Oil on panel. 114.5 x 89 cm

ANONYMOUS ARTIST FROM THE LATE 16TH CENTURY

Paintings from the circle of Marcus Geeraerts the Younger are marked by dryness, flatness and dark colour scheme but at the same time quite truly reflect the characteristics of the people from the epoch of Elizabeth I. The portrayed man demonstrates a cold and estranged aristocratic manner. The artist emphasizes the details revealing the social status of his model. His right hand rests on a helmet while his left hand touches the sword hilt, which makes the viewer guess he is a courtier and officer. The name of the man is unknown, yet his age (32) and the date of the portrait's creation are inscribed in the upper corner of the painting.

William Dobson. *Portrait of Abraham van der Doort.* Before 1640. Oil on canvas. 45 x 38 cm

WILLIAM DOBSON
1611–1646

Dobson was a most talented British portraitist from the 17th century. One of his best works is the likeness of the medal-maker and keeper of Charles I's art collections. Van der Doort was a loyal servant of his king, deeply devoted to him. He took great care of the royal treasures and committed suicide in 1640, when one of the most valuable miniatures he was in charge of was lost.

Cameo: *Portrait of Elizabeth I Tudor*
Circa 1560. Workshop of Julien de Fontenay (?).
Sardonyx and gold. 6.2 x 4.7 cm

The cameo came to the Hermitage from France in 1787 within the collection of Duc d'Orleans purchased by Catherine II. In its size and quality it surpasses five other Hermitage cameos portraying this powerful British queen.

GODFREY KNELLER
1648–1723

Kneller was a leading portrait painter in the late 17th – early 18th centuries. The Hermitage possesses two masterpieces by the artist – *Portrait of Grinling Gibbons* depicting a well-known sculptor and wood carver and *Portrait of John Locke* (1690s) that was executed shortly before the great philosopher's death.

Godfrey Kneller. *Portrait of Grinling Gibbons.* Before 1690. Oil on canvas.
125 x 90 cm

Wine-cooler. By Charles Kandler. 1734–35.
London. Silver; casting and chasing.
100 x 169 x 98 cm

This vast bowl used to cool bottles of wine is a unique piece of artistic casting which has no equals in other art collections all over the world. Its two galvanocopies are to be found in the Victoria & Albert Museum, London, and Metropolitan Museum, New York. It may have been acquired for Empress Anna Ioannovna.

Joshua Reynolds. *Infant Hercules Strangling the Serpents.* 1786–88. Oil on canvas. 303 x 297 cm

JOSHUA REYNOLDS
1723–1792

The first President of the Academy of Arts and most influential English painter of his time, Joshua Reynolds is revered in his homeland as a great portrait painter. He is represented in the Hermitage collection by four historical compositions, which are quite rare in his work. Reynolds's painting showing Venus and Cupid, the artist's replica of the famous work now at the Tate Gallery in London, can be classed as a mythological subject only with a great degree of reservation. Reynolds's Venus is a representation of a smart red-haired English model. This model might be Emma Hart, later the romantic and beautiful Lady Hamilton, who twice sat for the artist in her youth.

Joshua Reynolds. *Cupid Untying the Zone of Venus.* 1788. Oil on canvas. 127.5 x 101 cm

Thomas Gainsborough. *Portrait of a Lady in Blue.*
Late 1770s – early 1780s. Oil on canvas. 76 x 64 cm

THOMAS GAINSBOROUGH
1727–1788

Portrait of a Lady in Blue is a real gem of the Hermitage collection and the only canvas by Gainsborough, this poetic and refined genius of the 18th-century British school, owned by the museum. His painting is remarkable for a wealth of shades and a virtuoso craftsmanship, but at the same time his models are distinguished by a special refinement, poetic quality and elevated feelings.

JOSIAH WEDGWOOD
1730–1795

The Green Frog Service was commissioned to the outstanding pottery designer and manufacturer Josiah Wedgwood by Catherine the Great in 1773. It consists of 944 pieces, each featuring views of buildings and landscapes in various parts of England. It was intended for the Chesme Palace built by Yury Velten in 1774–77 between St Petersburg and Tsarskoye Selo – at the place called La Grenouillere, or Kekerekeksinen (Finnish: frog march), which explains the green frog emblem on every piece of the service.

Josiah Wedgwood.
Pieces from the Green Frog Service.
1773–74. Staffordshire.
Creamware; painting

George Romney. *Portrait of Mrs Harriet Greer.*
1781. Oil on canvas. 76 x 64 cm

GEORGE ROMNEY
1734–1802

George Romney was a well-known portraitist and younger contemporary of Joshua Reynolds and Thomas Gainsborough. He never rivaled them in his mastery yet was very popular among the London commissioners, ladies in particular. Freely and easily the artist conveyed the elegance, aristocratism, gracefulness and charm of his models, members of high society.

Joseph Wright of Derby. *Firework Display at the Castel Sant' Angelo in Rome.*
1779. Oil on canvas. 162.5 x 213 cm

JOSEPH WRIGHT OF DERBY
1734–1797

Joseph Wright of Derby is reckoned one of the most unusual English painters of the 18th century. In his *Iron Forge* the artist transforms the subject taken from real life into a romantic elegy. The focus of Wright's interest is a whimsical play of light and shade rather than people. The picture won a great popularity in England and was bought in the artist's studio specially for Catherine the Great.

Joseph Wright of Derby. *The Iron Forge Viewed from Without.* 1773. Oil on canvas. 105 x 140 cm

Benjamin West. *Venus Consoling Cupid Stung by a Bee.* Late 1790s. Oil on canvas. 77 x 64 cm

JOHN HOPPNER
1758–1810

Like George Romney, Hoppner had a great artistic skill and was a follower of Joshua Reynolds and Thomas Gainsborough. His portrait probably shows the famous playwright, orator and politician Sheridan, though there is no data that could prove that the author of the *School for Scandal* ever sat for him.

BENJAMIN WEST
1728–1820

An American by birth, Benjamin West settled in England when he was a mature professional artist. He borrowed the subject for his *Venus Consoling Cupid Stung by a Bee* from the *Wounded Cupid* ode by the Ancient Greek poet Anacreon. As a true adherent of Classicism, West carefully "reconstructs" ideal ancient images on canvas. However, the image of a crying Cupid and the light pink-bluish colour scheme lend to this scene a sentimental flavour.

John Hoppner. *Portrait of Richard Brinsley Sheridan (?).* Late 1780s – early 1790s. Oil on canvas. 77 x 64 cm

HENRY RAEBURN
1756–1823

Raeburn was a famous British artist of the 18th century. His friend Walter Scott was considered a symbol of Scottish literature and culture. Raeburn's portraits are laconic and restrained. Their main aim is to render the model's individual characteristics by using a well-devised colour scheme, contrasts of light and shade and expressive drawing.

Henry Raeburn. *Portrait of Mrs E. Bethune.* 1790s. Oil on canvas. 76 x 64 cm

GEORGE MORLAND
1763–1804

In the late 17th century landscape gained in importance in British art. *Approaching Storm* is held to be one of the best landscapes in Morland's huge but not always equally valuable output. In it Morland somewhat foresees Romantic revelations of the early 19th century.

George Morland. *Approaching Storm.* 1791. Oil on canvas. 85 x 117 cm

THOMAS LAWRENCE
1769–1830

Thomas Lawrence's glory of a portraitist went far beyond the borders of England. Almost all crowned persons, diplomats and army leaders of Europe thought it honourable to sit for the celebrated British master of portraiture. The Hermitage's portrait of Count Mikhail Vorontsov allows us to appreciate the exceptional talent of the artist capable to see behind outward effects and convey individual qualities of the model. A general who participated in the war against Napoleon and was wounded in the battle of Borodino, the future governor of the Novorossiysk Province, the count is represented here against the stormy sky, lit, as it were, by the romantic halo of a victor and hero.

Thomas Lawrence. *Portrait of Count Mikhail Vorontsov.* 1821. Oil on canvas. 143 x 113 cm

GEORGE DAWE
1781–1829

George Dawe was invited to Russia by Emperor Alexander I to paint a large series of portraits for the 1812 War Gallery. He was showered with commissions from the Russian aristocracy. His portrait of General Alexander Shishkov, an outstanding statesman, was not finished, yet it gives a true notion of the British artist's manner.

George Dawe. *Portrait of Alexander Shishkov.* Circa 1827. Oil on canvas. 103 x 78 cm

Christina Robertson. *Children with a Parrot.* 1850. Oil on canvas. 112 x 104 cm

CHRISTINA ROBERTSON
1796–1854

The well-known Salon artist Christina Robertson, a typical representative of the official Victorian style, had a large high-ranking clientele at the Russian court. She worked in the capital of Russia in the 1830s to 1850s. Painted in different countries, her portraits were all of the same type. Only minor details (like a Russian Orthodox church in the background of this painting) allow us to guess in what country her portraits were done.

RICHARD PARKES BONINGTON
1802–1828

A talented landscape innovator, Richard Parkes Bonington spent most of his short creative life in France. The artist deliberately preferred in his paintings commonplace views, ungainly corners. He endowed them with a strikingly convincing mood of calm and poetry and paid special attention to the rendering of light and colour effects. The works by Bonington laid foundation for the creative achievements of leading European landscape painters in the 19th century.

Richard Parkes Bonington. *Boats near the Shore of Normandy.* Circa 1825. Oil on canvas. 33.5 x 46 cm

French Art and Art of Other Western European Countries: 19th – 20th Centuries

THIRD FLOOR: ROOMS 314, 316–326, 333–350

The rooms of the Winter Palace third floor display the collection of Western European art from the 19th and 20th centuries. The collection of French art from the first half of the 19th century is uneven, yet represents many major French artists. Their works reflect a complex and dramatic struggle of ideas and movements characteristic of the period. Paintings by David demonstrate the basic principles of Neoclassicism. The influence of David is manifested in the works of his numerous pupils, such as Francois Gerard and Antoine-Jean Gros.

In the 1820s the rational Neoclassicism was replaced by the emotional and dynamic Romanticism, its illustrious representative being Eugene Delacroix. It was followed by Naturalism, or Realism; the Hermitage has landscapes of the Barbizon school that belong to this trend. The Barbizon artists Theodore Rousseau, Jules Dupre, Charles-Francois Daubigny and the remarkable landscapist Camille Corot set examples for the Impressionists Claude Monet, Pierre-Auguste Renoir, Edgar Degas, Camille Pissarro and Alfred Sisley. The creative searches of the great French sculptor Auguste Rodin make him largely close to Impressionism.

Cezanne opened a new page in the history of painting – Post-Impressionism. Its other representatives were Vincent van Gogh and Paul Gauguin who foreshadowed 20th-century art. Fauvism, the earliest art trend of the 20th century, owes its birth to Henri Matisse. The Hermitage boasts one of the richest in the world collections of Pablo Picasso's works. The museum collection representing major trends of French art from the second half of the 19th – early 20th centuries is justly regarded as one of the best outside France.

Exhibition of French Art: Late 19th – Early 20th Centuries. Matisse Room

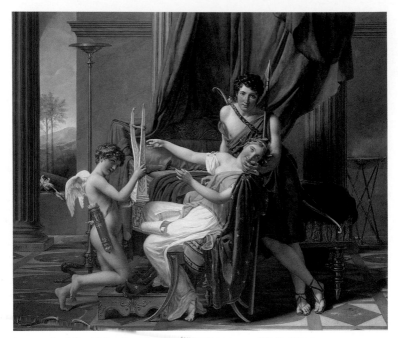

Jacques–Louis David. *Sappho and Phaon.* 1809. Oil on canvas, 225.3 x 262 cm

JACQUES–LOUIS DAVID
1748–1825

Like in the time of Nicolas Poussin, two centuries later, the artists turned to subjects and forms of Antiquity again. The leading figure of Neoclassicism was Jacques-Louis David. The Hermitage owns one of his pictures. David created *Sappho and Phaon* when he became court painter to the new French Emperor, Napoleon Bonaparte, whose reign became known as the First Empire. It gave its name to the style of the period – Empire style. The painting is based on a myth about Sappho, a famous Ancient Greek poetess, who fell in love with the young beautiful Phaon and committed suicide unable to bear the torments of unrequited love.

Francois Gerard. *Portrait of Josephine de Beauharnais.* 1801. Oil on canvas. 178 x 174 cm

FRANCOIS GERARD
1770–1837

Many of David's pupils could rival him in talent. Gerard was a recognized master of portrait painting who won great popularity among his clientele. In his large-scale *Portrait of Josephine de Beauharnais* the artist idealizes the appearance of Napoleon's first wife in keeping with the ideals of beauty born of a general infatuation with Classical Antiquity.

Antoine-Jean Gros. *Napoleon Bonaparte on the Arcole Bridge* (the author's replica of the original done in 1797). Oil on canvas. 134 x 104 cm

ANTOINE-JEAN GROS
1771–1835

Napoleon was a true hero for the representatives of Neoclassicism and they depicted him in a large number of their paintings. In *Napoleon Bonaparte on the Arcole Bridge* Antoine-Jean Gros, David's favourite pupil, who took part in the Italian campaign, shows the young French commander at the moment of triumph when the French Army is defeating the Austrian one at the Battle of Arcole.

JEAN-AUGUSTE-DOMINIQUE INGRES
1780–1867

The talent of Jean-Auguste-Dominique Ingres, the most significant figure in David's circle, was revealed during the years of the First Empire. Ingres showed himself a true innovator in portraiture and achieved absolute perfection in it. His only work in the Hermitage, *Portrait of Count Nikolai Guryev*, may be considered one of the best examples of this kind of painting.

Jean-Auguste-Dominique Ingres. *Portrait of Count Nikolai Guryev.* 1821. Oil on canvas. 106 x 86 cm

Ferdinand-Victor-Eugene Delacroix. *Lion Hunt in Morocco.* 1854.
Oil on canvas. 74 x 92 cm

FERDINAND-VICTOR-EUGENE DELACROIX
1798–1863

Two Hermitage paintings by Delacroix, ideological leader of French Romanticism, deal with the themes of mysterious East, fascinating for a European's imagination. The artist had made a journey to Algeria and Morocco as early as 1832, but even twenty years later his Moroccan impressions still inspired his ingenious and powerful paintings. Delacroix's *Lion Hunt in Morocco* is pervaded with energy and dynamism.

Ferdinand-Victor-Eugene Delacroix.
Moroccan Saddling His Horse. 1855. Oil on canvas. 56 x 47 cm

ANTOINE-LOUIS BARYE
1795–1875

The oeuvre of this celebrated animalistic sculptor is closely connected with Romanticism. Like painters adherent to this trend, he was fond of depicting passion outbursts and dramatic situations. His favourite material, bronze, was able to express all his ideas.

Antoine-Louis Barye. *Lion and Serpent.* 1832.
Bronze. Height 25 cm

FRANCOIS XAVIER WINTERHALTER
1805–1873

This French artist of German origin was court painter to King Louis-Philippe and later Napoleon III. His compositions display somewhat theatrical character. The accessories and attributes are no less important for the artist than the faces of his models.

JEAN-LEON GEROME
1824–1904

An illustrious representative of the Paris Salon, Gerome made a brilliant career and received all possible titles and prizes. His *Sale of a Slave Woman* gained a wide recognition at the 1884 Salon and was exhibited under the name *Slave Market in Rome*.

Francois Xavier Winterhalter.
Portrait of Sophia Naryshkina. 1858.
Oil on canvas. 150 x 114 cm

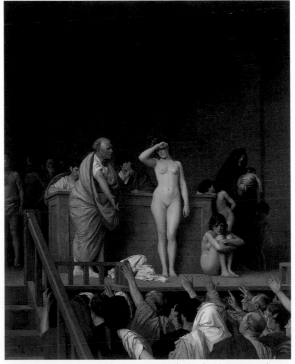

Jean-Leon Gerome. *Slave Market in Rome (Sale of a Slave Woman).*
Circa 1884. Oil on canvas. 92 x 74 cm

HIPPOLYTE (PAUL) DELAROCHE
1797–1856

Delaroche's impressive historical compositions gained him popularity. They combined fascinating romantic subjects with the impeccable mastership of execution. His works were pathetic, yet superficial in their interpretation of the subject.

Hippolyte (Paul) Delaroche. *Cromwell before the Coffin of Charles I.* 1848. Oil on canvas. 226 x 291 cm

NARCISSE–VIRGILE DIAZ DE LA PENA
1808–1876

A Spaniard by birth, Diaz was one of most popular artists of the Salon in the 1850s. Small paintings by this very talented master are distinguished by their rich colour scheme and romantic aura of the themes.

Narcisse–Virgile Diaz de la Pena. *Gypsies Listening to the Prophecies of a Young Fortune-Teller.* 1848. Oil on canvas. 104 x 78 cm

JULES–AIME DALOU
1838–1902

Dalou was a representative of the Naturalist trend in French sculpture. He supported the rebellion of the Paris Commune and after its fall emigrated from France for some time and lived in London. He created many large public monuments in Paris. The theme of motherhood was of particular importance for Dalou.

Jules–Aime Dalou. *Peasant Woman with Her Child.* 1873. Terracotta. Height 125 cm

Constant Troyon. *On the Way to the Market.* 1859. Oil on canvas. 260.5 x 211 cm

CONSTANT TROYON
1810–1865

Troyon was an eminent Salon artist and adherent of the Barbizon school. His simple country motifs enlivened with romantic feelings had such a great success that he was hardly able to execute all the commissions he received.

Theodore Rousseau. *Market-Place in Normandy.* 1832 (?). Oil on panel. 29.5 x 38 cm

THEODORE ROUSSEAU
1812–1867

Rousseau was a leading landscape painter of the Naturalist trend. He left Paris and settled in the village of Barbizon where he was joined by a number of his friends who shared his views. Thus the Barbizon school was formed that made a significant contribution to the development of a new type of French landscape painting.

JULES DUPRE
1811–1889

Dupre was one of the leaders of the Barbizon school that took interest in modest ordinary landscapes of the north of France. Like other members of the group, he spent long hours in the open air trying to render the effects of light.

Jules Dupre. *Landscape with Cows.* 1870s. Oil on canvas. 54 x 74 cm

JEAN-BAPTISTE-CAMILLE COROT
1796–1875

The artist's contemporaries described him as "magic Corot." His paintings permeated with light and lyrical feeling seemed to give "wings" to the viewer. He prepared the way for the Impressionists who learned much from him.

CHARLES-FRANCOIS DAUBIGNY
1817–1878

Daubigny was a famed French landscapist, representative of the Barbizon school. *Seashore at Villerville*, one of his best works, dates from the artist's late period and unites many of his painterly achievements.

Jean-Baptiste-Camille Corot. *Peasant Girl Grazing a Cow at the Edge of a Forest.* 1865–70. Oil on canvas. 47.5 x 35 cm

Charles-Francois Daubigny. *Seashore at Villerville.* 1875. Oil on canvas. 85 x 149 cm

Claude Monet. *Lady in the Garden (Sainte-Adresse).* 1867. Oil on canvas. 80 x 99 cm

Claude Monet. *Haystack at Giverny.* 1886. Oil on canvas. 61 x 81 cm

CLAUDE MONET
1840–1926

In 1874 the young artists Claude Monet, Auguste Renoir, Edgar Degas, Camille Pissarro and Alfred Sisley, not recognized by official criticism, decided to arrange their own exhibition. It was then that the word "Impressionism" was derived from Monet's painting *Sunrise at Le Havre. Impression* – a derogatory name that would later become the generally accepted title of this new trend in French art and express its main concept. Eight beautiful Hermitage paintings by Monet – from his early *Lady in the Garden* to *Waterloo Bridge*, created already at the beginning of the next, 20th century – illustrate the evolution of the creative manner of this artist, leader of the new generation of French painters.

Claude Monet. *Corner of the Garden at Montgeron.* 1876–77. Oil on canvas. 172 x 193 cm

Claude Monet. *Waterloo Bridge (Effect of Fog).* 1903. Oil on canvas. 65 x 100 cm

EDGAR DEGAS
1834–1917

The art of Edgar Degas cannot be entirely associated with Impressionism. Drawing in an academic vein, precise and clear, was always the main expressive means of his art. By no chance his idol was Ingres, a most famous artist of the first half of the 19th century. The Hermitage has a series of large pastels by Degas who is considered an unsurpassed master of this difficult medium.

Edgar Degas. *Woman Combing Her Hair (At the Toilet).* 1885–86. Pastel on cardboard. 53 x 52 cm

PIERRE–AUGUSTE RENOIR
1841–1919

The six paintings in the Hermitage collection demonstrate the best qualities of the art of this remarkable master. His brush captured his characters at different moments of their everyday life. The models posing for Renoir possessed some features in common allowing us to speak about a certain poetic generalization, a sort of "Renoir's" type of woman or child.

Pierre–Auguste Renoir. *Girl with a Fan.* 1881. Oil on canvas. 65 x 50 cm

Pierre–Auguste Renoir. *Boy with a Whip.* 1885. Oil on canvas. 105 x 75 cm

Pierre–Auguste Renoir. *Portrait of the Actress Jeanne Samari.* 1878. Oil on canvas. 174 x 101.5 cm

Alfred Sisley. *Village on the Seine, Villeneuve-la-Garenne.* 1872. Oil on canvas. 59 x 80.5 cm

ALFRED SISLEY
1839–1899

Alfred Sisley, an Englishman who was born in Paris, was fond of painting the city's picturesque environs. His canvas *Village on the Seine, Villeneuve-la-Garenne* wonderfully permeated with light is undoubtedly one of the most lyrical works of early Impressionism.

CAMILLE PISSARRO
1830–1903

Camille Pissarro was the oldest member of the Impressionist circle. His favourite subject was Paris which he painted in every season. His series devoted to Boulevard Montmartre consists of thirteen canvases painted by Pissarro from the window of his studio.

Camille Pissarro. *Boulevard Montmartre in Paris.* 1897. Oil on canvas. 73 x 92 cm

Paul Cezanne. *Smoker*. 1890–92. Oil on canvas. 92.5 x 73.5 cm

Paul Cezanne. *Still Life with a Curtain*. 1899. Oil on canvas. 55 x 74.5 cm

PAUL CEZANNE
1839–1906

The Hermitage collection of the great painter consists of eleven works exhaustively representing all the phases in the formation of his creative system that brilliantly revealed itself in still life, landscape and portrait paintings. The Impressionists' influence helped Cezanne to get rid of his dark colour range, although his canvases would never serve as examples of their artistic system. Cezanne evolved his own painterly principles. He rendered volumes and forms not by means of light and shadow as the Old Masters did, but by alternating warm and cold shades of colour. Pursuing his difficult aims, he consciously made up his still life compositions of objects that were simple in shape and allowed the painter to look for their underlying geometrical forms – the sphere, the cylinder and the cone.

Paul Cezanne. *Mont Sainte-Victoire*. 1900. Oil on canvas. 78 x 99 cm

Henri Rousseau. *In a Tropical Forest. Struggle between Tiger and Bull.* 1908. Oil on canvas. 46 x 55 cm

HENRI ROUSSEAU
1844–1910

Rousseau was an officer of the Paris custom-house, but his interest in painting was so great that he began painting himself. The three Hermitage paintings by this highly original and ingenious master who occupies a place apart in French art of the turn of the 19th and 20th centuries are superb examples of his naive art, most powerful and expressive.

PAUL SIGNAC
1863–1935

Signac was one of a number of artists who combined the spontaneity of Impressionism with the deliberation and precision of a carefully defined system and created a scientific method of separating complex tones into pure colours. Signac's *Harbour at Marseilles* is done in the pointillist technique which is based on the use of small dotted applications of paint.

Paul Signac. *Harbour at Marseilles.* 1906. Oil on canvas. 46 x 55 cm

Vincent van Gogh. *Ladies of Arles (Memory of the Garden at Etten).* 1888. Oil on canvas. 73 x 92 cm

Vincent van Gogh. *Lilac Bush.* 1889. Oil on canvas. 72 x 92 cm

VINCENT VAN GOGH
1853–1890

A Dutchman by birth, Van Gogh spent the most important and fruitful part of his short and tragic life in France. His divided stroke, combination of contrasting complementary tones and succulent palette from which pure white and black were eliminated were used not as a means to create an optical illusion of reality but to express his emotional state, his violent temperament. The Hermitage owns four works by Van Gogh which were painted during the last phase of his life, at Arles and at Auvers-sur-Oise.

Vincent van Gogh. *Cottages.* 1890. Oil on canvas. 60 x 73 cm

Paul Gauguin. *Tahitian Pastorals.* 1893. Oil on canvas. 87.5 x 113.7 cm

Paul Gauguin. *Woman Holding a Fruit.* 1893. Oil on canvas. 92 x 73 cm

PAUL GAUGUIN
1848–1903

Being a prosperous broker, Gauguin took up painting as an amateur. At the age of thirty-five he made his final choice and began a professional artistic career. He created his best works at Tahiti – an island of his dream, which he had sought for throughout his previous life and where he found a veritable earthly paradise inhabited by beautiful, natural and free people. Gauguin lived amidst the Tahitians more than ten years, almost to his death, remaining an unrecognized and misunderstood individualist rebel in his native country. The Hermitage boasts a large collection of Gauguin's paintings – fifteen works created mainly at Tahiti Island.

Paul Gauguin. *Sunflowers.* 1901. Oil on canvas. 73 x 92 cm

Pablo Picasso. *Two Sisters (The Meeting).* 1902.
Oil on canvas pasted on panel. 152 x 100 cm

PABLO PICASSO
1881–1973

Pablo Picasso. *Boy with a Dog.* 1905. Gouache
on cardboard. 57 x 41 cm

The Hermitage owns over thirty paintings produced by Picasso in the early stage of his career, after his arrival in Paris from Spain at the age of twenty. In 1902–04 the feelings of solitude, ennui, sorrow and suffering pervaded his paintings, which are considered to be works of the Blue period (the period owes its name to the artist's predilection for the blue colour). In 1906 Picasso arrived at Cubism, which developed from the heavy geometricized figures of the Analytical period to the more elaborate arrangements of the so-called Synthetic phase. The artist seems to have broken objects in order to make up of their fragments new, previously unseen constructions. An intellectual play of pure form, set free from the dictate of nature, takes place. The further development of this tendency led to the foundation of Abstract Art.

Pablo Picasso. *Woman with a Fan (After the Ball)*. 1908.
Oil on canvas. 152 x 101 cm

Pablo Picasso. Jug: *Man's Head (Bearded Man)*. 1953. Clay. Height 29 cm

Pablo Picasso. *Musical Instruments*. 1912.
Oil, plaster and sawdust on oilcloth. 98 x 80 cm

Henri Matisse. *The Red Room (Harmony in Red)*. 1908. Oil on canvas. 180.5 x 221 cm

Henri Matisse. *The Dance*. 1910. Oil on canvas. 260 x 391 cm

Henri Matisse. *The Painter's Family.* 1911. Oil on canvas. 143 x 194 cm

HENRI MATISSE
1869–1954

In 1905 in Paris opened an exhibition whose participants were dubbed the Fauves by art critics (French "fauves" means "wild animals") for their bold colours and sketchy manner. Henri Matisse was the recognized leader of the trend. The Hermitage has over forty paintings, along with drawings, collages and book illustrations, that cover every stage in the evolution of the artist.

Henri Matisse. *Portrait of the Artist's Wife.* 1913. Oil on canvas. 145.3 x 97.2 cm

Henri Matisse. *Henriette III (Large Head).* 1929. Bronze. Height 40 cm

MAURICE DE VLAMINCK
1876–1958

Matisse's friend who shared most of his views, Maurice Vlaminck passed a test with the Fauves and continued searching for his own manner. His landscapes are full of dramatic tension expressed in dynamic impasto brushstrokes and open combinations of different colour shades.

Maurice de Vlaminck. *View of the Seine.* Oil on canvas. 54 x 64.5 cm

AUGUSTE RODIN
1840–1917

Rodin's famous marble compositions suggest the changeable state of the world with no less intensity than paintings by the Impressionists. Light sliding over the rough surface of marble or bronze dissolves the outlines making his modelling of the shapes nearly as soft as in painting.

Auguste Rodin. *Eternal Spring.* Early 1990s. Marble. Height 77 cm

Auguste Rodin. *Age of Bronze.* 1870s. Plaster. Height 173 cm

Andre Derain. *Portrait of an Unknown Man with a Newspaper (Chevalier X).* 1914. Oil on canvas. 162.5 x 97.5 cm

ANDRE DERAIN
1880–1954

Andre Derain had passionately shared Matisse's ideas, but soon resolutely turned to Cubism. Worthy of special mention among his fourteen Hermitage works is the *Portrait of an Unknown Man with a Newspaper* which brought together many diverse tendencies including his interest in African sculpture and early mediaeval painting.

KEES VAN DONGEN
1877–1968

Kees van Dongen, who had arrived in Paris from Holland, became a fashionable portrait painter introducing the public at large to a mysterious, extravagant and vicious world of the Parisian artistic Bohemians. He created his own distinctive type of a Parisian woman, vividly and sharply reflecting in a special way the aesthetic ideal of the early 20th century.

Kees van Dongen. *Woman in a Black Hat.* Circa 1908. Oil on canvas. 100 x 81.5 cm

Albert Marquet. *Bay of Naples*. 1909. Oil on canvas. 62 x 80.3 cm

ALBERT MARQUET
1875–1947

The work of Albert Marquet, in comparison with the mighty colourful symphonies of his friend Matisse, seems to be intimate and traditional. Like the Impressionists, Marquet sought to render a transparent atmosphere pervaded with light but his painting is more conventional and balanced.

RAOUL DUFY
1877–1953

Dufy contributed to the Fauves' exhibitions and in the 1920s became a favourite artist of high society salons. His work is distinguished by an ease and virtuoso elegance of execution, and a wonderful gift as a colourist. These qualities are equally visible in his large-scale decorative paintings, fabric designs and easel paintings. His *Regatta*, now in the Hermitage collection, is also remarkable for its high artistic merits.

Raoul Dufy. *Regatta (Yachts in the Port of Dauville)*. Circa 1936. Oil on canvas. 54 x 80.8 cm

Chaim Soutine. *Self-Portrait with a Beard.* 1916. Oil on canvas. 54 x 30.5 cm

CHAIM SOUTINE
1893–1944

Soutine was an Expressionist of the so-called Paris school. He came to France from Russia in 1913. His work comprises landscapes, portraits and still lifes. His artistic manner is highly individual. Though his themes are often tragic, his painting is energetic and cheerful.

FERNAND LEGER
1881–1955

Leger worked in the media of book illustrations, mosaics, coloured glass and stage-sets. He was in charge of large-scale decorative projects all over the world. Leger took interest in the theories of movement and mechanics. Parts of the human body often look in his works like tubes, motors and gears.

Emile-Antoine Bourdelle. *Eloquence.* 1917. Bronze. Height 17 cm

EMILE-ANTOINE BOURDELLE
1861–1929

Bourdelle is the author of a monument to the hero of the Argentine liberation movement, General Carlos Maria Alvear, in Buenos Aires. He produced not only the sculpture but also the architectural design for the monument's grandiose twenty-two-metre high construction. The Hermitage head *Eloquence* is a study for the statue of the same name showing an orator.

Fernand Leger. *Postcard.* 1932–48. Oil on canvas. 92.3 x 65.4 cm

GIORGIO MORANDI
1890–1964

Morandi is one of most unusual modern Italian artists. He received education at the Bologna Academy of Fine Arts. Since his young years he had been interested in the work of French innovators. The refined works of the mature artist, two of which are to be seen in the Hermitage, betray the influence of Cezanne and 17th- and 18th-century Neoclassical painting.

Giorgio Morandi. *Still Life.* Late 1920s. Oil on canvas. 51 x 57.5 cm

Massimo Campigli. *Seamstresses.* 1925. Oil on canvas. 161 x 96. 5 cm

MASSIMO CAMPIGLI
1895–1971

An Italian by birth, Campigli had no art education. When living in Paris he saw Cubist works by Picasso and Leger. On taking a professional artistic career he advocated a return to the traditional representational monumental art. His works combine an Avant-garde search with the influence of Etruscan painting and frescoes by Giotto, Masaccio and Piero della Francesco.

RENATO GUTTUSO
1912–1987

This Italian painter ranks among the most remarkable 20th-century masters. His artistic manner and worldview were formed under a strong influence of Eugene Delacroix, Francisco Goya, Theodore Gericault and Honore Domier as well as Expressionism and Cubism. His oeuvre belongs to the Neorealist trend.

Renato Guttuso. *Portrait of Rocco and His Son.* 1960. Oil on canvas. 136 x 113 cm

FRANCESCO MESSINA
1900–1995

The work of Messina holds a place apart in the Italian sculpture from the middle of the 20th century. Inspired by best national traditions, he, together with Giacomo Manzu and Emilio Greco, brilliantly embodied the ideals of the Italian sculpture of his time in his works.

Emilio Greco. *Large Sitting Figure*. 1973. Bronze. Height 133 cm

EMILIO GRECO
1913–1995

This Italian sculptor had a lyrical talent. His work was oriented towards Classical art heritage. Most of his sculptures are nude female figures. He chose models of a certain type: they must have had an elongated neck, sloping shoulders and a smoothly lined silhouette. He preferred to show sharp twists of the body and turns of the head which made his figures look dynamic.

Francesco Messina. *Beatrice*. 1959. Bronze. Height 145 cm

GIACOMO MANZU
1908–1991

An outstanding Italian sculptor, Manzu was a recognized leader of this art form in the 20th century. He was strongly influenced by Auguste Rodin. His work is characterized by the symbolical generalization of forms. His models, a bit awkward and angular, are highly spiritual. He is famous for his compositions done for the doors of St Peter's Cathedral in Rome.

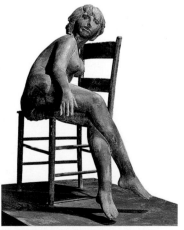

Giacomo Manzu. *Tebe Seated*. 1983. Bronze. Height 125 cm

AUGUSTO MURER
1923–1991

A Venetian monumental sculptor, Murer took part in the Resistance during World War II and later designed many antifascist monuments set in the cities of Northern Italy. He also depicted mythological characters of Antiquity and commedia dell'arte personages. An exhibition of his works was mounted in the Hermitage in 1982. To express his gratitude to one of the largest art institutions in the world Murer presented six of his statues to the museum.

FERNANDO BOTERO
Born 1932

This Columbian sculptor belongs to the "traditional grotesque" trend, close to naive art. His objects have exaggerated forms as if being swollen with self-satisfaction. He has been actively working since 1973 creating all sorts of variations of similarly excessive forms. His ironic-heroic monumental compositions have been installed in many cities of the world.

Augusto Murer. *Faun with a Flute.* 1980. Bronze. Height 195 cm

Fernando Botero. *Still Life with a Water-Melon.* 1976–77. Bronze. Height 109 cm

Ignacio Zuloaga. *Dwarf Gregorio.* 1908. Oil on canvas.
187 x 54 cm

IGNACIO ZULOAGA
1870–1945

This Spanish artist was influenced by Edouard Manet and Henri de Toulouse-Lautrec as well as the tradition of his own country, mainly Diego Velazquez and Francisco Goya. He is considered to be the founder of modern Spanish genre, portrait and landscape painting. His works are marked by a rich colour scheme and expressiveness.

ROCKWELL KENT
1882–1971

The work of this American artist is distinguished by its severe spirituality, precise powerful outlines and unique colour scale. He produced oil paintings, watercolours, lithographs etc. He was a traveller and politician.

Rockwell Kent. *Early November. Northern Greenland.* 1933. Oil on canvas pasted on plywood. 85 x 112 cm

Russian Culture: 9th – 19th Centuries

SECOND FLOOR: ROOMS 151, 153, 155–190

The Winter Palace rooms display rich collections of the Department of Russian Culture. Paintings, sculptures, works of applied art created in this country fit well into the palatial interiors which are objects of special pride, outstanding examples of Russian architecture in their own right.

The Russian Culture Department is the youngest one in the Hermitage. It was set up in 1941 and comprised collections transferred to the museum from the Museum of the Ethnography of the USSR Peoples, Artillery Museum, Museum of the October Revolution and Pavlovsk Palace; later its collections constantly grew. Since the 1950s the Department regularly sent scientific expeditions to most distant parts of the country. Many of the icons, specimens of folk art, manuscripts and old printed books found in the expeditions were on the verge of complete destruction and were saved by the Hermitage restorers. The most ancient items dating from the 6th century were discovered by the Department staff in the cause of archaeological excavations.

The collection of early Russian icons is relatively small, yet it illustrates fairly well the main Old Russian schools of icon painting – those of Moscow, Novgorod, Pskov and North of Russia. A real masterpiece of the Novgorod school from the 16th century is *St Nicholas of Zaraysk with Scenes from His Life*; noteworthy is the icon *St John the Theologian in Silence* and many others.

The Hermitage's collection of Russian painting from the 18th to early 20th centuries has a specific character since many of these works were created or acquired for the decoration of the Imperial residence. The battle scenes used to adorn the state and memorial rooms, likenesses of the Russian emperors and their families were mainly commissioned for the Romanov Portrait Gallery. The Department of Russian Culture also has portraits of statesmen and clergy, merchants and travellers, many of which were painted by the celebrated Russian artists Ivan Nikitin, Alexei Antropov, Fyodor Rokotov, Ivan Vishniakov and Dmitry Levitsky.

**Exhibition of Russian Culture:
First Half of the 18th Century**

Sts Theodore Stratelates and Theodore the Tyro. 15th century. Novgorod. Tempera on board. 53.5 x 38 cm

This iconographic type showing the saints at full length was widespread in Novgorod art in the 15th – 16th centuries. Theodore Stratelates and Theodore the Tyro were revered in Novgorod as holy soldiers and great martyrs who had given their life for Christ. In the upper part of the icon is the half-length representation of Jesus Christ.

The Virgin. Late 15th – late 16th centuries. Novgorod. Tempera on board; gilding. 158.5 x 60.5 cm

In the Deesis tier of the iconostasis representations of the Virgin of this type were set to the right of Christ. The Virgin is traditionally shown at full length in the attitude of prayer. The delicate features of her face, her small elegant hands and elongated figure make the icon close in type to the traditional works of the Moscow school from the 15th century.

St Nicholas of Zaraysk with Scenes from His Life. First half of the 16th century. Novgorod. Tempera on board; gesso-ground. 165 x 115 x 3 cm

The representation belongs to the icon type depicting St Nicholas, Bishop of Myra in Lycia, at full length with his arms spread out; the right hand blesses the viewer, the left one holds the Gospel. The fourteen border scenes feature episodes from St Nicholas's life. Though the icon has a Byzantine prototype, its saturated succulent colours are characteristic of the Novgorod school.

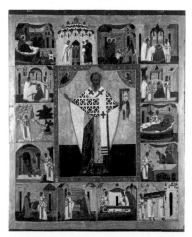

St John the Theologian in Silence. 1679.
By Nektary Kuliuksin. Workshop of the St Cyril
of Belozersk Monastery. Tempera on board.
109 x 85 cm

The Apostle John, Christ's
favourite disciple and the author
of the Gospel, three Epistles and
the Apocalypse, is represented in
the state of a deep concentration
contemplating the Divine Truth.
The gesture of the apostle's
right hand touching his mouth is
a sign of silence, while the left
hand of St John points to the
Gospel text. Depicted above the
apostle's shoulder is the figure
of the speaking Angel – the
personification of the Holy Spirit
and a symbol of the Divine Wisdom.

**Royal Doors with the *Annunciation* scene
and two holy hierarchs.** Late 16th – early 17th
centuries. Tempera on board. 148 x 77.5 cm

The Royal Doors are the main
entrance to the sanctuary (altar
part) in Orthodox churches. Some
of their stylistic traits betray their
origin from the Russian North.
Sts John the Chrysostom and Basil
the Great depicted here played a
great role in the history of Orthodox
Christianity. They wrote texts of
liturgies held daily in Orthodox
churches.

ANDREI MATVEYEV
1704–1739

In 1717 Matveyev was sent to study in Holland by Catherine I. In The Hague he was apprenticed to the painter Carel de Moore, which is proved by Matveyev's copy of Moore's portrait of Peter the Great. For his achievements Matveyev was made court painter by his patroness.

ALEXEI ZUBOV
1682 – after 1750

Andrei Matveyev. *Portrait of Peter I.* After 1725. Copy of Carel de Moore's original. Oil on canvas. 78 x 61 cm

In accordance with the order of the emperor, the artists of Peter I's time record in their works all the stages of St Petersburg's construction. They depicted separate buildings and views of the new capital's ensembles as well as most important events in its history.

Many engravings, Zubov's famous *Panorama of St Petersburg* among them, were done on the emperor's personal commission for diplomatic gifts.

Alexei Zubov. *Panorama of St Petersburg.* 1716. Etching with line engraving. 79 x 243 cm

Battle of Poltava. 1722. After L. Caravaque's cartoon. Imperial Tapestry Manufactory, St Petersburg. Woven by Philipp Behagle and I. Kobylyakov. Wool and silk. 300 x 315 cm

This is one of the earliest tapestries made in Russia, a fine example of decorative art from the first quarter of the 18th century. Battle scenes were a new type for Russian painting inspired by the country's victories in the Northern War. However, this tapestry is rather a formal portrait where the battle scene serves only as background reminding the viewer of the significance of Peter I's reign for Russia.

Peter I's travelling medicine chest.
Circa 1613–15. Germany, Augsburg. By masters Tobias Loyker and Hans George Brenne. Wood, copper, steel, silver, glass, silk, velvet and galloon; oil on copperplate, veneered with ebony and gilded. 39.5 x 41 x 32.5 cm

The Hermitage possesses collections of drawing and medical instruments which Peter I used in his everyday work. Noteworthy is the medicine chest, sort of a "mobile pharmacy."

Goblet in the form of a boat. 1706. Silver; casting, gilding and chasing

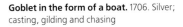

This goblet was made from newly-minted silver in the Nerchinsk Region, Siberia. Mounted on the prow of the boat is the figurine of a rearing lion that holds a horn in its mouth used for pouring wine. The boat was a favourite image in Peter's time and a symbol of the young Russian Empire.

Turning machine for copying medals.
1710 – early 1720s. Russia. St Petersburg (?). By master Franz Singer. Wood, steel and copper alloys. 144 x 185 x 150 cm

The Hermitage copying lathes and machines from Peter I's reign (all in all there are twelve in the collection) are various models of turning and copying devices. They were designed and made at the Turnery, Peter I's favourite workshop at the court, where the emperor would spend his pastime.

IVAN NIKITIN
1680s – 1742

The portrait of Peter I's daughter, Grand Duchess Elizabeth Petrovna (1709–1761), Future Empress Elizabeth (since 1741), is the earliest of the extant eighteen works by the court painter of Peter I, Ivan Nikitin. The luxurious formal attire of the child which consists of a heavy low-necked dress and ermine mantle covering her shoulders were required by the court etiquette.

Ivan Nikitin. *Portrait of Elizabeth Petrovna as a Child.* Circa 1712. Oil on canvas. 54 x 43 cm

BARTOLOMEO CARLO RASTRELLI
1675–1744

The work of Bartolomeo Carlo Rastrelli introduced Russian sculptors to the European artistic tradition and laid foundation for the national school of sculpture. His pieces housed in the Hermitage begin the history of Russian secular sculpture. These include the bust of Alexander Menshikov (1717), two busts (bronze and wax, the latter dates from 1719) of Peter I, posthumous wax figure of Peter I (1725) and others.

Bartolomeo Carlo Rastrelli. *Portrait of Emperor Peter I.* 1723–29. Bronze; casting, chasing and engraving. 102 x 90 x 40 cm

IVAN VISHNIAKOV
1699–1761

A celebrated Russian artist who produced portraits, monumental and decorative paintings and a representative of the Rococo style, Vishniakov headed the Painting Team of the St Petersburg Construction Office. The wedding portrait of the wife of a well-known St Petersburg merchant done by Vishniakov still looks like a *parsuna* (the term derived from the Latin word *persona* describes a type of portrait painting that developed in Russia in the late 16th century and was, in a sense, a transition between traditional icon painting and the more Westernized "realistic" portrait). At the same time it has many traits of a secular European painting.

Ivan Vishniakov. *Portrait of Stepanida Yakovleva.* After 1756. Oil on canvas. 90 x 72 cm

MIKHAIL LOMONOSOV
1711–1765

Lomonosov made a substantial contribution to the art of mosaics. For long years he had been developing a special technique for making mosaics of coloured glass pieces. His mosaic works were recognized by the Academy of Arts of which he was elected a member.

Mikhail Lomonosov. *Portrait of Peter I.* 1755–57. After the original of Johann Gottfried Tannauer. Mosaic; smalt. 89 x 69 cm

ALEXEI ANTROPOV
1716–1795

Antropov was a prominent Russian portrait painter. He also produced many monumental decorative compositions and was member of the Academy of Arts. The likeness of the priest Fyodor Dubyansky, spiritual counselor of Empress Elizabeth Petrovna, have features of both old-fashioned *parsuna* and secular portrait.

Alexei Antropov. *Portrait of Fyodor Dubyansky.* 1761. Oil on canvas. 99.5 x 76.5 cm

IVAN ARGUNOV
1727–1802

Argunov was a remarkable portrait painter active in the middle of the 18th century. He was a serf artist of Count Pyotr Sheremetyev, one of the wealthiest men of his time, owner of the famous Fountain Palace in St Petersburg and estate of Kuskovo near Moscow. His father Filed Marshal Boris Sheremetyev, close associate of Peter the Great, had been the first nobleman in Russia to receive the title of count.

Ivan Argunov. *Portrait of Boris Sheremetyev.* 1760. Oil on canvas

Snuff-box with pug-dogs. 1752. Imperial Porcelain Factory. St Petersburg. By Dmitry Vinogradov. Porcelain and gold; overglaze polychrome painting. 4.7 x 6 x 6 cm

Since Peter I's time the Russians had been striving to find the secret of true porcelain. It was a talented mining engineer Dmitry Vinogradov who worked out the composition of porcelain paste. Its quality was in no way inferior to that of Saxon porcelain and its composition, in which only Russian raw materials were used, was similar to the Chinese paste. In 1744 Empress Elizabeth Petrovna founded the first in Russia porcelain manufactory, later known as Imperial Porcelain Factory.

ANONYMOUS ARTIST FROM THE SECOND HALF OF THE 18TH CENTURY

This likeness is considered to be a rare private portrait of Catherine II painted during her trip to the conquered Crimea. It differs from the empress's formal portraits in the realistic interpretation of the model: her face shows signs of aging and her travelling dress is of a simple design.

Anonymous artist from the second half of the 18th century. *Portrait of Catherine II in a Travelling Dress.* Circa 1787. Oil on canvas. 52.2 x 65.8 cm

CARL LUDVIG CHRISTINECK
1730/32 − circa 1794

The portrait depicts an illegitimate child of Catherine II and her favourite Count Grigory Orlov. Bobrinsky was actually a half-brother of future Emperor Paul I. The artist creates a charming image of the young aristocrat who has a tender pretty face and open and pure look.

Carl Ludvig Christineck. *Portrait of Count Alexei Bobrinsky as a Child.* 1769. Oil on canvas. 90 x 73.5 cm

Johann–Baptist Lampi I. *Portrait of Prince Alexander Bezborodko.* 1794. Oil on canvas. 121 x 95 cm

JOHANN–BAPTIST LAMPI I
1751–1830

Johann-Baptist Lampi I was an Austrian painter who lived and worked in Russia. He was a virtuoso painter of formal portraits. One of them represents Prince Alexander Bezborodko, participant of the Russian-Turkish wars, statesman, art patron and collector.

MINA KOLOKOLNIKOV
Circa 1708 – circa 1792

Kolokolnikov ranks among the best Russian portraitists of the 18th century. This representation of a young nobleman with a round shining face having a healthy and fresh look of the one living a simple country life is a most noteworthy work by the painter.

Mina Kolokolnikov. *Portrait of a Young Nobleman.* 1780s. Oil on canvas. 95 x 73 cm

Vladimir Borovikovsky. *Portrait of Grand Duchess Yelena Pavlovna.* Before 1799. Oil on canvas. 72 x 58 cm

VLADIMIR BOROVIKOVSKY
1757–1825

An artist of great lyrical talent and portraitist who took special interest in the feelings and state of mind of his models, Borovikovsky was the leader of Russian Sentimentalism which came into fashion in the late 18th century. The formal portraits of six daughters of Paul I convey an atmosphere of tenderness and dreaminess.

Clock in the form of an egg.
1769. By Ivan Kulibin

This clock of the size of a goose egg was presented by Ivan Kulibin to Empress Catherine II who was so much impressed by this self-taught engineer that appointed him the head of the mechanical workshop at the St Petersburg Academy of Arts. The clock was equipped with a chiming mechanism that played a variety of melodies and another mechanism that set the tiny figures of the miniature theatre to motion.

Pieces from the St George Order Service.
1778. Fyodor Gardner's factory. Porcelain; gilding and overglaze polychrome painting

The St George Order Service for eighty persons was first used during the formal dinner given at the Winter Palace to mark the ninth anniversary of the Order's institution. The principal motifs of the decoration are a ribbon interwoven with a garland of laurels and the star of the Order. The service was designed on the basis of the Berlin Service presented to Catherine II by Friedrich II.

Casket for storing chessmen and chessmen.
1780s. Tula. By master Adrian Sukhanov. Steel and bronze; faceting, polishing, burnishing and gilding. 17 x 50 x 31 cm

The casket was presented to Catherine II. The lid has a representation of the unfulfilled reconstruction of the Tula Armoury. The sides show the figures of Glory and Athena. The decor employs Classical motifs: laurel wreaths and acanthus leaves. The casket holds eighty chessmen.

Chair of the Grand Master of the Maltese Order with a footrest. Between 1798 and 1800. To a design of Giacomo Quarenghi. Wood and velvet with silver lace and fringe (original upholstery); carving and gilding. 156 x 115 x 96 cm

This is the throne of Paul I who in 1790 became the Grand Master of the Maltese Order. It was part of the furniture set from the Maltese Chapel built in 1798–1800 by Giacomo Quarenghi next to the Vorontsov Palace granted by the emperor to the knights of the Order.

Carnival sleigh with the figurine of St George. Russia. 1760s. Wood, steel, leather, velvet and gold leaf; carving. 174 x 350 x 116 cm

Sleigh riding was a most popular winter pastime of the royal court in the 18th century. The astonished foreign guests described in detail the boisterous Shrovetide (Mardi Gras) celebrations attended by Peter I and his family. To mark the signing of the Peace of Nystad, in accordance with the emperor's order, an entire Russian fleet, consisting of boats, yachts and other vessels was put on sleighs driven by horse and "sailed" up and down the snow-covered streets of Moscow. The Imperial sleighs would be abundantly decorated with carved figures and ornaments and gilded. To celebrate the coronation of Catherine II a grandiose carnival "Triumphant Minerva" was held on the streets of Moscow during the Shrovetide week. For three days a procession went up and down the streets representing, in tune with Catherine's idea, the social vices put an end to by her wise reign.

Art of Ancient Egypt and Asia Minor

FIRST FLOOR: ROOMS 88–90, 100

The Hermitage collections of relics representing the culture and art of the peoples of the East are large and varied, as is the East itself. These collections reflect the age-long paths traversed by different Eastern peoples and civilizations, some of which have disappeared, while others have survived to the present day. The collections have been formed on the basis of geographical and historical characteristics of this very large region of the world. The relics of ancient Egypt, Mesopotamia, Assyria and Palmyra, covering the period from the 4th millennium BC to the 4th century AD, illustrate the most ancient history of this immense region.

◄ **Exhibition of the Art of Ancient Egypt and Asia Minor**

Relief representing King Ashurnasirpal II accompanied by his deity–guardian.
883–859 BC. Assyria. Limestone.
Height 243 cm, length 217 cm

This relief comes from the palace of the Assyrian ruler at Kalakh (the capital of the Assyrian state in the 13th – 11th and 9th – 8th centuries BC). The image of the king holding a bow and arrows is to demonstrate the might of this powerful state's ruler.

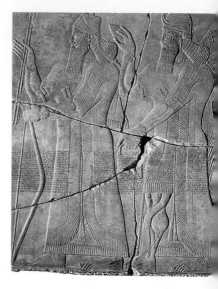

Stele of Ipi. Second half of the 14th century BC. New Kingdom, XVIIIth Dynasty. Ancient Egypt. Limestone. 95 x 71 cm

This stele represents Ipi, "great overseer of the royal household" and royal scribe of Pharaoh of Egypt, Tutankhamen, worshipping a statue of Anubis, god of embalming and protector of the dead. Well preserved are the colours, blue and green, made from lapis-lazuli and malachite.

Statue of the goddess Sekhmet–Mut.
Mid-14th century BC. New Kingdom, XVIIIth Dynasty. Ancient Egypt. Granite.
Height 200 cm

It is one of the 600 statues of the goddess that were set in the temple complex on Asheru Lake by the order of Pharaoh Amenhotep III. Daughter of the sun god Re, Sokhmet ("powerful") depicted as a ferocious lioness was revered as the goddess of the broiling sun and fierceness of war.

Sculpture of Amenemhet with his wife and mother. Late 14th – early 13th centuries BC. New Kingdom, XVIIIth Dynasty. Ancient Egypt. Basalt

The sculpture dates from the period following the fall of the religious reform of Akhenaton (Pharaoh Amenhotep IV). It is not by chance that the representation of the people is accompanied by the text of prayer from the Book of the Dead. The Egyptians used to decorate their tombs with such funerary sculptural groups.

Statuette of a priest. Mid-14th century BC. New Kingdom, XVIIIth Dynasty. Ancient Egypt. Wood. Height 14.5 cm

This small wooden figure of a priest is a real masterpiece of the Hermitage collection of ancient Egyptian art. According to the ancient Egyptian canon, the priest is shown walking. Originally his hands held some attributes which are now lost. Such statuettes were widespread in the New Kingdom period.

Statue of Amenemhat III. 19th century BC. Middle Kingdom, XIIth Dynasty. Ancient Egypt. Granite. 86.5 cm

This statue of Amenemhat III (19th century BC, XIIth Dynasty) is the only fully preserved royal stone sculpture in the Hermitage collection of ancient Egyptian art. The conventional representation, done in the traditional idealizing style, manifested the might and unconquerable power of the pharaoh.

Art of Central Asia and the Caucasus

FIRST FLOOR: ROOMS 46–52, 55–63, 66, 68, 69

A notable place in the Hermitage collection is held by a large number of diverse exhibits covering the thousand-year-old creative activities of the peoples of Central Asia (4th millennium BC – 20th century) and the Caucasus (10th century BC – 19th century). The excavations of Penjakent and Varaksha, started in 1947 and going on nowadays, have revealed to the world an almost unknown before, highly developed civilization of Sogdiana.

The Hermitage rooms display inimitable mural paintings (5th – 6th centuries) from the palaces of these two ancient cities on the territory of Central Asia. The Hermitage restorers have saved these superb masterpieces of mediaeval art from inevitable destruction.

Represented in the Hermitage collection is also the unique culture of one of the most ancient states that existed on the territory of present-day Armenia in the 9th – 6th centuries BC – Urartu.

Exhibition of the Art of Central Asia.
◀ **Fragment of mural painting from the Red Hall**

Figure of a deity. Part of the throne decoration. 8th – 7th centuries BC. Toprak-Kale, Armenia. Bronze. Height 16 cm

Feasting Man. Fragment of mural painting from the Blue Hall. 8th century. Sogdiana, Penjakent. Plaster and glue paints

Such figures formed the decoration of a large throne made for one of the rulers of the state of Urartu. These threatening fabulous creatures, sometimes shown with bared teeth, were intended to protect Urartian rulers against evil forces and to impress ambassadors from other countries, emphasizing the richness and power of Urartu.

Feast scenes in the mural paintings of Sogdiana echo Sassanian motifs. In this piece the artist masterfully conveys a quiet dignity in the posture of the feasting man and the elegant movement of his hand accentuated by the lifted wine-bowl.

Snow Leopard Hunt **scenes.**
7th – 8th centuries BC. Fragment of mural painting from the Red Hall. Sogdiana. Plaster and mineral pigments. Height 150–200 cm

Demons. Fragment of mural painting from the Blue Hall. 8th century. Sogdiana, Penjakent. Plaster and glue paints

This piece gives a notion of the decor of one of the state rooms in a palace of the ruler in the Bukhara oasis. It features several recurrent motifs rhythmically arranged on an intense red background. A hunter (probably a legendary king), seated on an elephant, fights against beasts attacking him on either side – snow leopards, tigers and gryphons.

This piece surpasses all the extant Penjakent murals in its great mastery. One of the scenes represents a legendary hero (probably, Rustam whose feats are described in the poem *Shahnameh* by Firdawsi) fighting a single combat with fantastic creatures.

Byzantine Art and Art of the Near East

THIRD FLOOR: ROOMS 381–397

The exhibition of Byzantine art and culture which was inextricably linked with the East in the 4th – 15th centuries is to be found on the third floor of the Winter Palace. The rooms next to it display art works from mediaeval Iran, Syria, Turkey and other countries of the Near East. They were created between the 1st millennium BC and 19th century. Iranian art holds a place apart in the wide panorama of art from the Near East. The gem of the Hermitage Museum is a unique collection of silver from the Sassanian era (3rd – 7th centuries) unparalleled anywhere in the world. It comprises over fifty vessels, dishes, bowls etc discovered in different parts of Russia, mostly by chance. These fine specimens of silverwork demonstrate great sophistication and virtuosity of technique.

◀ **Exhibition of Byzantine Art**

St Gregory Thaumaturgus. 12th century.
Byzantium.Tempera on board. 81 x 53 cm

This icon is one of the most important examples of Byzantine painting and best exhibit of the type in
the Hermitage collection. St Gregory
Thaumaturgus (the Wonderworker)
(circa 221 – circa 270) is one of the
most revered saints. He is known as
the author of the Creed which, according to tradition, was given to
him by the Virgin (Theotokos) and
St John the Evangelist.

Christ the Pantocrator. 1363. Byzantium.
Tempera on board. 106 x 79 x 2.8 cm

Icons of this type are traditionally
set in the centre of the Deesis tier
of the iconostasis or in the top of
the church dome. The Gospel which
Christ holds in his left hand indicates
his mission – annunciation of the
"good news" (gospel).

Angel. 6th century. Byzantium.
Stone and smalt (tesserae)

Mosaic was the main technique
employed for Byzantine
monumental compositions.
This Hermitage piece has much
in common with the celebrated
Ravenna mosaics which are dated
to the reign of Emperor Justinian
marked by the first flourishing
of Byzantine art.

Dish of Bishop Paternus. 498. Byzantium. Silver and gold; chasing, engraving and gilding. Diameter 61 cm

The Latin inscription running along the border mentions Paternus who was the bishop of Thoma (modern Constanza) in the late 5th – early 6th centuries. The reverse of the dish has hallmarks which allow establishing the exact date of its production.

Lamp. Body. Second half of the 10th century. Rock crystal. Egypt; Mounting. Late 16th century. Gold and enamel. Italy. Height 26.5 cm, length 22 cm

Lamps were invented dozens of thousands years ago. They were vessels (for oil) made of pottery or metal with apertures or a spike to support the wick and control the rate of burning and wick itself. This traditional shape was long used.

Diptych with circus scenes. 5th century. Byzantium. Ivory; carving. Height 33 cm

According to tradition, in the 5th and 6th centuries such ivory diptychs were produced to commemorate the conferment of the title of consul, an important event celebrated with a circus performance. That is why the two panels show animals being taunted. There is, however, no sign of the traditional representation of a new consul.

Bucket. Late 12th – early 13th centuries. Iran, Herat. Bronze (brass), silver and copper; gilding, casting, forging and decoration with inlay. Height 18.5 cm

People of the East would spend much time in baths. The tradition originates in Antiquity when thermae had been very popular. Many everyday objects used as bath utensils impress us with their elegance and lavish decor.

Dish: King Shapur II Hunting Lions. 4th century. Iran. Silver; chasing, engraving and gilding. Diameter 22.9 cm

Silver and golden bowls, dishes and other vessels were the pride of Iranian princes and the nobility who settled all major problems during feasts. The decor of silverware combined various technical devices: casting with subsequent forging, damascening, chasing, engraving and gilding. As for representations, there was a limited repertory of subjects and a compositional canon both in portraits of the kings and in the depiction of triumphal battles and victories.

Dish. 16th century. Turkey, Isnik. Faience; painting

It is a typical work from the town of Isnik, largest Turkish centre of pottery production. Motifs of tulip and carnation done in the intense blue, turquoise, red and green colour scheme were most popular in the works from Isnik.

Vase with representation of a polo game.
13th century. Iran. Faience; painting with lustre.
Height 80 cm

This is a masterpiece of pottery from the period. The composition of the glaze employed for their production included metal salts or silver producing a characteristic mother-of-pearl sheen. The pieces were burnt in the final stage. This technique was later borrowed by Spanish potters.

Ewer with representation of two peacocks.
5th – 6th centuries. Iran. Bronze (brass); casting and chasing. Height 38 cm

Widespread in mediaeval Iran were utensils made of metal, often precious metal, which contradicted the Koran. Most of them have been lost, only some bronze items survive. It was in that period that first decorative statuettes appeared; they depicted birds and animals. The same subjects were popular in pottery.

Aquamanile in the form of an eagle.
796–97. Iran (?). By master Sulaiman. Bronze (brass), silver and copper; casting and chasing. Height 38 cm

This is the earliest precisely dated bronze piece of the Islamic period. The Eastern countries had always had a special attitude to water, yet it was Islam that created a whole cult of ritual purity and ablutions before prayers. Water also had associations with gardens, an indispensable element of Islamic notions about paradise.

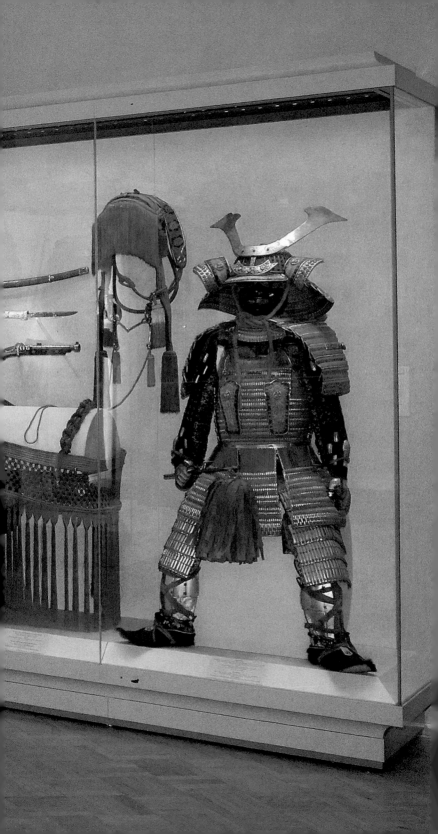

Art of the Far East

THIRD FLOOR: ROOMS 351–370

The countries of the Far East, especially China, Japan and Indonesia, are represented by articles ranging from the 3rd millennium BC to the 20th century.

China, the country of ancient traditions with a history of three and a half millennia, occupies a prominent place in the displays of the Department of the East. Fine specimens of mediaeval art from the 6th – 10th centuries, including loess sculptures, were found by the expedition of Sergei Oldenburg in the Buddhist monastery of Qian-fuo-dong ("The Cave of a Thousand Buddhas") in close vicinity of the town of Dunhuang in 1914–15. Over three hundred art works from the 12th – 13th centuries were discovered by the archaeological expedition led by Pyotr Kozlov in 1908–09 and 1926 in the cause of excavations of the ancient town of Kharo-Khoto. The Hermitage collection was enriched with paintings done on paper, silk and linen as well as woodblock prints. Chinese art of later periods is mostly exemplified by a large collection of porcelain which has always been appreciated as an unsurpassed achievement of Chinese art and culture. The Hermitage also possesses lacquers, pieces of carved stone, enamels and unique works of applied art marked by great mastery.

◀ **Exhibition of the Art of the Far East**

Head of the Buddha's Disciple.
8th century. Fragment of the *Passing of the Buddha* (?) mural painting. China, Dunhuang, the Cave of a Thousand Buddhas. Mineral pigments. 60 x 44 cm

This masterpiece of the Hermitage's Chinese collection is dated to the T'ang dynasty (618–907), the golden age of Chinese culture. The face of the Buddha's lamenting disciple is delightful for the mastery of its execution and expressiveness. All artistic means, including light-and-shade modelling, characteristic of some trends in Chinese portrait painting of this period, are used to emphasize an emotional tension of the scene.

Head of Devata. 6th – 7th centuries. China, Xinjiang, Karashar. Clay and loess. Height 19.5 cm

It is an example of sculpture from the T'ang dynasty period. The statues made of loess portray not only handsome young boddhisatvas with round faces but also evil spirits – entrance guardians, demons – and temple donors depicted in luxurious dress.

The Buddha Amitabha Meeting the Soul of the Righteous Man on the Way to the Pure Land. 12th century. China, Khara-Khoto. Mineral pigments on linen. 142.5 x 94 cm

The cult of the Buddha Amitabha is one of most popular in China. It was believed that those who venerated the deity were reborn to live in his Pure Land, or paradise, after their death. Shown against the bright background of the sky is the lord of the "pure land" accompanied by two bodhisattvas who carry the lotus throne which is to play a certain role in the rebirth of the righteous. The deceased monk is represented as a naked boy standing on a cloud.

The Boddhisatva Mahasthamaprapta. 13th century. China, Khara-Khoto. Mineral pigments on silk. 125 x 62.5 cm

The Khara-Khoto painting is characterized by the interaction of two different traditions – Chinese and Tibetan. The latter which does not strictly adhere to the canon is represented by the image of Boddhisatva Mahasthamaprapta.

Portrait of an Official and His Wife.
15th – 16th centuries. China. Indian ink and mineral pigments on silk. 143 x 106 cm

It is a rare specimen of the Chinese ritual portrait associated with the ancestor cult. The man is wearing the suit of a 4th-rank official: a hat of a particular design and red gown embroidered with birds; his wife is also wearing a gown of the same colour and a scarf.

Portrait of a High Official. 12th century. China, Khara-Khoto. Indian ink on paper. 45 x 32 cm

It is an example of traditional Chinese painting from the Sung dynasty period. It displays a psychological characteristic of the model, restrained colour scheme, precise silhouette and elegant lines.

Dish with lotuses. Diameter 36.3 cm

Dish with peonies. Diameter 34.5 cm

Basin for fish. Diameter 36.9 cm; height 33 cm

Porcelain pieces with "famille verte" type of painting. Late 17th – early 18th centuries. China

The development of the production techniques of famous Chinese porcelain took centuries. In the 17th century overglaze painting was introduced which allowed creating polychrome decorations in a wide variety of colours. The typical colour scheme dominated by bright green tones gave its name ("famille verte," or "green family") to an entire group of porcelain pieces.

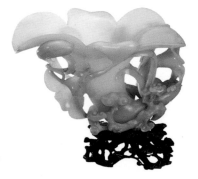

Porcelain pieces with cobalt painting. China

The Hermitage has a representative collection of porcelain dating from the 14th – 18th centuries. Before the 17th century kilns were of a simpler design, good only for the production of porcelain decorated with cobalt painting which could withstand high temperatures.

Vase in the form of a pomegranate twig with a large flower. 18th century. China. Jade and wood; carving and polishing. Height 20 cm

Bowl on a ring-shaped foot. Second half of the 16th century. Height 16 cm; diameter 32.5 cm

Since ancient time jade had been regarded as a sacral material; it used to play a ritual role and symbolize the state power. In the 15th – 19th centuries it began to be employed rather for decorative purposes, in the production of jewellery and table ornaments.

Octahedral vessel. 16th century. Height 27.7 cm

*The **Buddha Maravijaya.*** Between 1378 and 1438.
Siam (now Thailand), Sukhothai. Bronze.
Height 42.5 cm

The Hermitage's Thai collection represents all the schools active from the 14th till 19th centuries. Buddha Maravijaya (Buddha overcoming Mara, the prince of Dark) was a most popular type of representation in Siam. This sculpture is an example of the post-classical period of the art of Sukhothai (the first Thai state) that had developed a specific iconographic canon of the Buddha's image, which came to be known as the Kampheng Phet type (after the name of a city in central Sukhothai).

Set of boxes. 18th century.
China. Wood; black and golden lacquers

The production of lacquers is one of most ancient crafts in China. They were widely used in all spheres of life – from kitchen utensils to arms and exterior decorations. There are three types of lacquers: painted, carved and decorated with inlay. Since the 18th century these techniques are mixed in the production of lacquered objects.

Netsuke

The collection of netsuke (carved toggles) dating from the 17th – 19th centuries is a most valuable part of the Japanese art displays. It consists of over one thousand pieces and boasts works by most prominent carvers and from all known schools. The subjects are traditional for this type of art.

Hotei and Karako. Late 18th – early 19th centuries. Netsuke. Japan, Kyoto. Ivory; carving. 3.9 x 4 cm

Fukurokuju. Late 18th – early 19th centuries. Netsuke. Japan, Osaka. Ivory; carving. 4.8 x 3.7 cm

Hsui Pei-hung. *Cat.* Indian ink on paper

HSUI PEI-HUNG
1895–1953

Traditional Chinese painting is represented by a small number of works, yet their quality is beyond praise. The most noteworthy are works by the celebrated artists of the first half of the 20th century Hsu Pei-hung and Chi'i Pai-shih, done in the "gokhua" style.

Horseman and His Servants. Second quarter of the 17th century. India. Mughal school. Mineral pigments on paper. 37 x 28 cm

The miniature features a horseman wearing costly clothes who belonged to the ruling Mughal dynasty, which is testified by a green-gold orb. He is accompanied by his servants carrying a large fan made of peacock feathers and an emblem showing the sun.

Archaeology of Eastern Europe and Siberia

FIRST FLOOR: ROOMS 11–33

Rooms on the first and third floors of the Winter Palace house the collection of primitive culture. The Department of the Archaeology of Eastern Europe and Siberia was set up not so long ago – in 1931. Nevertheless, first exhibits, objects discovered by archaeologists in the excavations of hundreds of barrows built by the nomad tribes roaming the southern parts of Russia, began to arrive into the Imperial collection as early as the reign of Catherine II. The vast territories of the country had a great number of burial mounds left by ancient peoples that had been superseding one another for centuries. The most noteworthy are those of the Scythians that held priceless treasures. The Scythians were nomads who came to the southern Russian steppes in the 8th – 7th centuries BC from the Iranian highlands. They had no written language, yet the finds from the Scythian barrows give a notion of their customs, traditions, religion and everyday life.

In the middle of the 19th century Peter I's Siberian collection of gold objects that had been kept in the Kunstkammer (Chamber of Curiosities) since 1726 was transferred to the Hermitage. 20th-century scholars have found out that all these objects were made between the 7th century BC and 1st century AD by the nomad tribes of the Saka, a people related to the Scythians.

The sensational discoveries connected with the culture of ancient nomads of Southern Siberia and the Altai Mountains, the stone choppers of the Lower Palaeolithic (about 400,000 years ago) found on the territory of Armenia, the wooden and bone articles form the Neolithic settlement discovered in the Shigir peat bog near Yekaterinburg, the stone slabs with incised mysterious petroglyphs brought by the Hermitage expedition from the bank of Lake Onega and many other artifacts rank with the most famous exhibits of the museum.

Exhibition of the Department of the Archaeology of Eastern Europe and Siberia

Female figurine. Mid-20th millennium BC. Voronezh Region, village of Kostenki. Limestone. 10.2 x 4 cm

The earliest works of art are the so-called "Venuses", female statues executed during the Upper Palaeolithic age. The women's faces had no interest for the ancient craftsman whose attention was attracted to those parts of the woman's body with which her genital functions were connected: a huge bulging belly, rounded hips and breasts.

Female figurine. Circa 20th millennium BC. Irkutsk Region, settlement of Malta. Mammoth ivory; carving, polishing and engraving. Height 13.4 cm

For the wealth and variety of artifacts from the Stone Age the Malta site ranks with the best in the world. The Eastern Siberian "Venuses", unlike their European counterparts, have schematically rendered figures with apparently distorted proportions, but their heads and faces are worked very thoroughly.

Slab with Onega petroglyths. 4th – 3rd millennin BC. Onega Lake, Pery Nos near the village of Besov Nos. Granite. Length 308 m; width 240 cm

Some scholars think that the images incised on the slab record the annual economic cycle of the ancient inhabitants of Karelia. Others regard the drawings as mythological scenes connected with the sun worship (circles and semicircles) and the cult of ancestors (boats with men).

Idol of Galich. Second half of the 2nd millennium BC. Kostroma Province, village of Turovskoye. Bronze; casting. Height 14 cm

The figurine of a sitting man with a disproportionally large head, narrow chest and nine radiating shoots was intended to be put on a rod. Together with a few other objects of this type, some silver pieces and coins, it forms the so-called Galich hoard.

Binocular-shaped vessel. Second half of the 3rd millennium BC. Chernovtsy Region, settlement of Polivanov Yar. Height 21.5 cm

It consists of two hollow bowls linked together by three crosspieces. The entire surface is covered with an elegant spiral-shaped ornament. Such vessels may have been used in rites. It is an example of the Tripolye Culture.

Head of a Female Elk. 3rd – 2nd millennia BC. Central Urals, Shigir peat bog. Elk horn; polishing. Length 19.5 cm

It is one of the best sculptural pieces from the Neolithic period, marked by liveliness and realism in the interpretation of the animal. It may have served as decoration of a vessel handle or ritual staff. The surface is polished; it may have been done in the process of usage.

Figurine of a seated woman. Early 3rd millennium BC. Southern Turkmenia, settlement of Yalangoch-Depe. Clay. Height 19 cm

This figurine is a typical specimen from the Eneolithic period. This nude woman has a bird-shaped head and square shoulders; the arms are mere stumps and the legs are simply indicated by a line. There are remains of pigments on the surface, probably the figurine was painted.

Terminal in the form of a large gryphon's head with a deer's head in its beak. 5th century BC. Eastern Altai, 2nd Pazyryk barrow. Wood and leather. Height 27 cm

The piece may have formed part of a male headdress, probably indicating the wearer's high status, expressed in the gryphon, repeated three times. Overall, the selection of elements, motifs and technical devices is typical of the Altai masters.

Bowl with handle in the form of a bear. 6th – 7th centuries. Komi Republic. Birch wart; carving. Height 8.5 cm. Detail

A special place in the Vanvizdino culture is held by the objects made in the so-called Perm animal style which reflected the cosmogonic myths and worldview of ancient people. The symbols of the upper world were heavenly elks, bears and birds.

Pile carpet. 5th – 4th centuries BC. Eastern Altai, 5th Pazyryk barrow. Felt; applique work. 640 x 450 cm. Fragment

The excavation of the 5th Pazyryk barrow in the Altai Mountains carried out in 1949 undoubtedly ranks with the most sensational discoveries of the 20th century. The archaeologists found under a burial mound a cell with a five-metre-long coffin. The sarcophagus contained the mummified corpses of the chieftain and his concubine. Outside the coffin were many objects including a chariot, corpses of nine horses and others. This pile carpet must have served as a side of the burial tent.

Swan.
5th – 4th centuries BC. Eastern Altai, 5th Pazyryk barrow. Felt; applique work. Height 30 cm

Such figures of white swans with black funeral strips marking their lowered wings would be attached to long poles used to support the burial tent.

Chariot. 5th – 4th centuries BC. Eastern Altai, 5th Pazyryk barrow. Wood and leather. Height 300 cm, diameter of wheel 150 cm

Thanks to the permafrost, the chariot is in an excellent state of preservation. It consists of a number of parts joined together by leather straps and wooden nails. It was made for a funeral ceremony. When discovered, it was dismantled.

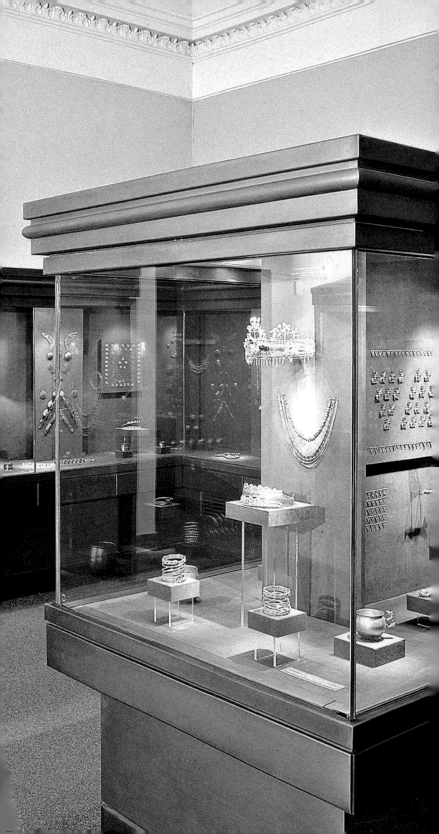

The Treasure Gallery 2

FIRST FLOOR

Today the Hermitage boasts a unique collection of jewellery ranging from ancient pieces produced as early as the Bronze Age to 20th-century works fashioned by Russian and foreign jewellers. The collection is split into two parts and displayed in two galleries (Treasure Gallery 1 in the New Hermitage and Treasure Gallery 2 in the Winter Palace), access to which is limited. The first two rooms of the Treasure Gallery 2 house gold objects unearthed in the excavations of barrows located on an enormous territory — from the Northern Black Sea littoral and Caucasus to the Urals and Eastern Siberia. The Treasure Gallery 2 exhibition starts with items from Peter I's Siberian collection, the first collection of gold objects from ancient barrows in Russia. Done in the animal style they mostly come from the Saka tribe burials. These are followed by specimens of Scythian art. The real gem of the gallery is the plaque in the form of a deer, found near the Kostromskaya stanitsa (village). No less famous is the Greek comb from the Solokha barrow, in the Dnieper area. Many of the precious ornaments discovered in the necropolises of once flourishing cities of Ancient Greek and Roman colonies demonstrate the unsurpassed mastery of their jewellers. The last part of the Treasure Gallery 2 exhibition features jewellery from the East. It also contains diplomatic gifts presented to the Russian emperors and empresses. Made in China, Turkey, Byzantium and Central Asia in the 18th — early 20th centuries, they display a breathtaking variety of forms and lavish ornamentation.

◀ **Exhibition of The Treasure Gallery 2**

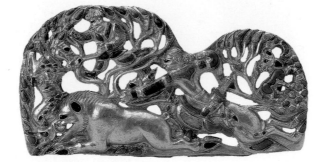

Belt plaque: *Wild Boar Hunt.* 6th − 5th BC. Peter I's Siberian Collection. Gold, corals and glass; chasing. Length 19.2 cm

It displays a superb decorative quality characteristic of genuine masterpieces of jewellery art. The plaque shows the hunting of a wild boar in the wooded and mountainous area.

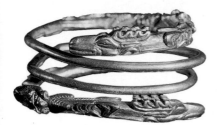

Bracelet with beasts of prey tearing at a stag. 1st century BC. Vologda Region, village of Verkhneye Pogromnoye. Gold; casting and forging. Diameter 8.4 cm

The motif of beasts of prey tearing at their victim used for the decoration of this spiral-shaped bracelet reflects the nomad's sacral worldview. The theme may have been borrowed from the art of Achaemenid period (Iran).

Comb: *Scythians in Battle.* Late 5th − early 4th centuries BC. Dnieper steppe area, Solokha barrow. Gold; casting, chasing and engraving. Height 12.3 cm

The comb with perfectly modelled figures of Scythian warriors has the shape of an ancient temple's pediment. It must have been fashioned by a Greek craftsman on the commission of a Scythian ruler.

Plaque: *Deer*. Early 6th century BC. Krasnodar Region, Kostromskaya stanitsa (village). Gold; casting and chasing. Length 31.5 cm

It was a shield decoration once. This fine specimen of the Scythian animal style is a highlight of the collection and the Hermitage's well-known emblem.

Plaque: *Panther*. Late 7th century BC. Krasnodar Region, Solokha barrow. Gold; casting and chasing. Height 32.6 cm

Panther is a popular motif in Scythian art. Making use of the stylization, typical of the animal style technique, the jeweller has expressed the nature of the beast, its guile, craft and caution.

Overlay for a *gorytos*. 4th century. Dnieper area near Nicopol, Chertomlyk barrow. Gold; stamping and chasing. 46.8 x 27.3 cm

Gorytos (case for a bow and arrows) was part of a warrior's traditional equipment. Discovered in the Chertomlyk barrow, this *gorytos* overlay has turned out to be one of most significant finds highlighting the history of Scythian art.

Funerary mask of a king. 3rd century (?).
Kerch, Pantikapaion necropolis. Gold; chasing.
22.5 x 15 cm

This portrait-mask of the Bosporus
king Reskuporid is a masterpiece
of Greek metalwork from the 3rd
century. It is the only known gold
funerary portrait found on the
Bosporus necropolises.

Earrings: *Nike in Quadriga.* Second half of
the 4th century BC. Theodosia. Gold; chasing
and filigree. Height 9 cm

It is one of most noteworthy works
by Greek jewellers. It owes its fame
to the technique that had reached
its acme in Athens at the time
delicate lacelike ornamental work
consisting of groups of tiny metal
balls.

Diadem. 1st century BC. Novocherkassk,
Khokhlach barrow. Gold, turquoise, corals,
garnet, pearls and amethyst; chasing.
Length 61 cm; height 15 cm

The diadem is considered a gem
of the Novocherkassk hoard.
The upper part has a frieze with
representations of trees and
animals; pendants are attached to
the lower part; in the centre is a
refined female head carved of rose
quartz by a Greek craftsman.

Vessel: *Scythian Warriors.* 4th century BC. Kerch, Kul-Oba barrow. Electrum; chasing. Height 13 cm

Temple pendant: *Nereid Carrying an Armour to Achilles.* 4th century BC. Taman Peninsula, Bolshaya Bliznitsa barrow. Gold; chasing. Height 13.5 cm

It is part of the funerary headgear of a priestess of Demeter. The exact purpose of such twin pendants, either attached to diadems or worn on the chest, is unknown. They have been found only in the barrows of the Northern Black Sea littoral.

It is one of most noteworthy specimens of Ancient Greek metalwork unearthed on the territory of the Northern Black Sea littoral. It is an important source for studies of Scythian everyday life.

Flask and dish. 17th century. Great Mughals dynasty. India. Gold, diamonds, rubies and emeralds; chasing and engraving. Flask's height 26 cm, dish's diameter 19.7 cm

The Hermitage collection of the Indian jewellery from the 17th century is probably the only one outside India. Most notable are twenty pieces from the diplomatic gift sent by the Iranian ruler Nadir Shah to the Russian Empire in 1741.

The Small Hermitage

History and Architecture

The building of the Small Hermitage – the next edifice after the Winter Palace in the line of buildings running along the Palace Embankment – was created by the two gifted architects, Jean-Baptiste Vallin de la Mothe and Yury Velten who brilliantly realized Catherine's wish to have one more, little palace intended for pastimes in the circle of friends and choice guests. Vallin de la Mothe was the author of the architectural project. In tune with his idea, the complex was to consist of two pavilions joined by galleries and a hanging garden laid down on the second-floor level between them. Velten realized the project creating an imposing Classical edifice perfectly matching the Baroque Winter Palace by Rastrelli and forming a single ensemble with it.

**Southern Pavilion
of the Small Hermitage**

◀ **Northern Pavilion
of the Small Hermitage**

Hanging Garden

In 1764 Yury Velten began construction of the Hanging Garden. Simultaneously with its creation the architect erected in the building's southern part a pavilion for the empress's favourite Count Grigory Orlov and linked it by a passageway with Catherine's private apartments in the Winter Palace opposite it. The pavilion was known as the "Nearby Home" and sometimes as the "Favourites' Block." Later, when it became the dwelling place of members of the Imperial family and major court dignitaries, it came to be called the Southern Pavilion of the Small Hermitage.

In 1769 Velten erected the La Mothe, or Orangery, Pavilion at the opposite end of the Hanging Garden. Here, at the level of the second floor, were the Orangery, a "hall with two windows," five studies and the hermitage (French: "a retired place") proper. This was a room, with a special device for raising tables from the lower floor, where "small hermitages" or entertaining parties, during which the hostess was on equal terms with her guests, took place. Catherine the Great was fond of these private soirees during which dinners were followed by reading, conversations, performances and games. From

The Hanging Garden

The garden had paths lined with white marble statues. Here trees were planted in tubs covered with lead and filled with earth, and flowerbeds were laid out. Along its perimeter the terrace of the garden was decorated with carved trelliswork which concealed the possessions of the "Semiramis of the North" from curious glances. The light metal screen stretched over this little garden made it possible to keep various singing birds and even small exotic animals there in summer. In winter, snow hills were arranged in the Hanging Garden for the empress and her guests who could enjoy tobogganing here.

The Pavilion Hall

The Pavilion Hall has been basically preserved intact till nowadays. This magnificent formal room faced with white marble combines the Renaissance motifs with exquisite details of Moorish architecture in its elegant decor. The openwork arcades, two-tiered colonnades of white Carrara marble, reliefs, gilded stucco mouldings, elegant

Peacock **clock**

railings of the upper galleries and a unique copy of an ancient mosaic ceiling, all adds to the beauty of this interior which ranks with the most impressive halls and rooms of the entire museum. The hall is divided into cosy corners adorned with sculptures, columns, Oriental fountains with drops of water falling noiselessly, like tears, from marble shells (the "Fountain of Tears"). On the side of the Hanging Garden Stakenschneider attached to the Pavilion Hall, in memory of the Orangery which had once been there, the Winter Garden and covered it with a glazed tent-shaped ceiling. In the centre, amidst evergreen exotic plants, he installed a marble fountain executed by the Italian sculptor Felice de Fovo. In 1939 the romantic Winter Garden was demolished. The hall houses a collection of so-called mosaic tables from the 18th and 19th centuries; their tops are made in the Florentine and Roman mosaic techniques.

The *Peacock* clock

The famous *Peacock* clock created in the 18th century by the English master craftsman James Cox was acquired by Prince Grigory Potemkin and brought to St Petersburg in a dismantled state. Only in 1792 the famous Russian craftsman Ivan Kulibin succeeded in assembling and setting the sophisticated mechanism in motion.

that period onwards the palace was called the Small Hermitage. It kept the name even after the total reconstruction of the Northern Pavilion which completely changed its appearance. In 1850–58 the architect Andrei Stakenschneider replaced old rooms of Catherine's period with a stunning Pavilion Hall.

However, the empress conceived to use the new palace not for amusements alone, but also as the museum of Imperial art collections. The first collection of Western European paintings acquired by Catherine from the Berlin merchant Johann Ernest Gotzkowski in 1764, together with some other collections, was displayed in the two picture galleries joining the pavilions of the Small Hermitage. The Western Gallery was renamed into Romanov Gallery when the portraits of the Romanov family members were exhibited here in the middle of the 19th century. The Eastern one became known as Peter I Gallery. Today the former houses collections of Western European applied art and Netherlandish painting from the 15th – 16th centuries.

Pavilion Hall

Western European Applied Art of the Middle Ages

FIRST FLOOR: ROOM 259

In Europe interest in collecting works of Western European applied art began to develop in the second half of the 19th century. The core of the Hermitage collection was formed by the items of artistic crafts bought by Alexander Basilewski in 1884. Part of his acquisitions found their way to the Hermitage. In the autumn of 1921 the museum opened the first permanent exhibition displaying relatively few yet extremely beautiful works covering all the types of applied art from the Romanesque and Gothic periods.

Pride of place among the specimens of mediaeval applied art is held by objects ornamented with cloisonne enamel. Thanks to the multi-coloured vitreous enamel paste filling the metal cells, the caskets, reliquaries and panels have a festive decorative look. In the 10th − 12th centuries there were several centres of enamel production, the most famous of them being Limoges. First workshops usually opened at monasteries and convents made mostly objects for religious use. Later workshops were set up in towns. The growing interest in Limoges enamels stimulated introduction of new types of objects manufactured there. Limoges ware included wash-hand basins, overlays for caskets, boxes, jewellery cases etc. The Hermitage collection is poor in mediaeval monumental sculpture and painting; yet its collection of modest works of applied art fashioned by anonymous craftsmen gives a comprehensive notion of the art from the period.

Exhibition of the Western European Applied Art of the Middle Ages. Romanov Gallery

Aquamanile in the form of a knight blowing a horn and holding a Norman shield, with a cheetah on the horse back. 3rd century. Hungary (?). Bronze; casting and chasing. Height 27 cm

It is one of the best exhibits in the collection of artistic bronzes. Aquamaniles (Latin: "aqua" – "water" and "manus" – "hand") were vessels shaped as fantastic or real animals and used by priests and landlords for ceremonial hand washing.

Monstrance. 1474. Estonia, Revel. Silver and glass; chasing, engraving and gilding. Height 112 cm

In the Roman Catholic Church the monstrance is a vessel in which the Eucharistic Host or relics are carried. Monstrances often had the shape of a tower with a cylindrical glass container inside. The tower was crowned by a roof with spires. Such vessels were introduced after the establishment of the Corpus Christi feast in 1264.

Statuette: *Seated Madonna and Child.* Early 14th century. France. Ivory; carving. Height 27 cm

Since the middle of the 13th century ivory carving became one of most favourite Gothic forms of applied art; it gained special popularity in Paris. The widespread cult of the Madonna gave an impetus to the creation of numerous statuettes depicting the Holy Virgin Mary wrapped in a very long cloak with heavy folds.

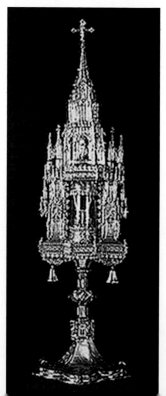

Reliquary with scenes from St Valeria's life.
Circa 1170. France, Limoges. Wood, copper
and cloisonne enamel; engraving and gilding.
Height 19.5 cm, length 22.7 cm, width 11.7 cm

It is a masterpiece of the collection
of Limoges enamels. It was
fashioned to mark the mystical
engagement of Richard I, the Lion
Heart, and the patron saint of
Limoges Valeria in 1170. According
to legend, Valeria who had adopted
Christianity under the influence
of St Marcialus, who baptized the
people of Limoges, brought her
head to her teacher after she had
been beheaded for Christ.

Tapestry: *Deer Hunt.* 15th – early 16th centuries. Germany. Wool, silk and gold threads;
weaving. 77 x 87 cm

It is the earliest fragment of a mediaeval tapestry from the Hermitage collection. The rider embodies
the ideal of the Lady Beautiful typical of mediaeval secular art. The deer
she is following stands for loyalty in
the symbolic amorous language. Such
tapestries were hung on the walls of
feudal castles.

Fortuni Vase. Mid-14th century. Spain,
Malaga. Faince; painting with lustre. Height
117 cm. Support. 19th century. Bronze

This very large glazed vase with
metallic lustre was used for storing
water or wine. It belongs to the so-
called Spanish-Moorish (Hispano-
Moresque) pottery. The vase was
produced in one of the major
mediaeval pottery centers, Malaga,
ruled at the time by the Arabs
who had conquered the Iberian
Peninsular in the 8th century. Its
body is covered with inscriptions
in Arabic containing good wishes;
its flat handles have a magic sign
"hand of Fatima" which was to
guard the contents of the vase.
The lower part of the vase has no
ornaments because it was dug into
the earth. It is inserted into a four-
leg support made after
the drawing of the
famous Spanish
artist Mariano
Fortuni who had
found the vase
in 1871.

Netherlandish Art: 15th – 16th Centuries

SECOND FLOOR: ROOMS 258, 261, 262

The Hermitage's collection of Netherlandish art of the 15th and 16th centuries comprising about one hundred paintings cannot claim for an exhaustive completeness, yet possesses a number of fine examples. Worthy of special note among several works by the Old Netherlandish Masters acquired by the Hermitage during the reign of Catherine the Great was the triptych, the *Healing of the Blind Man of Jericho*, by Lucas van Leyden, which came from the collection of Pierre Crozat. The major part of the Netherlandish paintings appeared in Russia thanks to 19th-century art collectors. One of them was the diplomat Dmitry Tatishchev whose collection joined the Hermitage in 1845. A gem of Tatishchev's collection was a diptych by Robert Campin. Another large collection, which came to the Hermitage in 1915 as a bequest of the well-known Russian geographer and traveller Pyotr Semionov-Tien-Shansky, also included several works by old Netherlandish artists.

The history of Netherlandish art is inseparably linked with the history of the country. In the 15th century the Netherlands, or the Low Countries, the territory lying in the lower reaches of the rivers Rhine, Maas and Scheldt, became part of the Hapsburg Empire (Holy Roman Empire). Since 1556 the country was ruled by King Philip II of Spain. A favourable geographical position and an advanced state of crafts and trade promoted the development of Netherlandish cities and towns that led in turn to the flowering of arts. In the 15th century the Netherlandish school of painting, the highest achievement in the culture of this small country, began to take shape. Unfortunately the destiny of many works created in this brilliant period of Netherlandish culture was quite dramatic. Some of them have been lost during wars, fires and religious feuds. Many altarpieces and sculptures were destroyed during the period of Protestant iconoclasm directed against the Catholic Church and its symbols.

In the 16th century, as the result of its close ties with Italy, Netherlandish art, underwent serious changes and began to acquire an increasingly secular character. New types of themes were introduced. In the late 16th – early 17th centuries the Netherlands ceased to exist and independent Dutch and Flemish schools of art began to be formed.

◀ **Exhibition of Netherlandish Art:
16th – 17th Centuries. Romanov Gallery**

ROBERT CAMPIN
Circa 1380–1444

Representative of the early Netherlandish painting, Robert Campin was the founder of the national school. One of his best works is the Hermitage's diptych. The right-hand wing depicts the Virgin, who is shown as a fair-haired Netherlandish woman with a baby in her hands; the scene is set in the interior of a burgher home. At the same time the artist endows many details of the real world with a hidden symbolic sense: the ewer and the towel, for example, allude to the innocence of the Virgin Mary and the sky seen through the window suggests the unseen presence of God.

ROGIER VAN DER WEYDEN
Circa 1400–1464

Robert Campin. *The Virgin and Child by a Fireplace.* 1430s. Right-hand wing of a diptych. Oil on panel. 34.3 x 24.5 cm

Rogier van der Weyden was Campin's most famous pupil. The picture is based on a legend that the Evangelist St Luke painted a likeness of the Virgin and Child when he had a vision of them. In connection with this legend St Luke was considered to be the patron of artists who often made him resemble themselves in their pictures. The story of this work is quite unusual. When the picture was in a Spanish monastery it was cut into two parts. The right-hand part with the figure of the Evangelist was acquired for the Hermitage in The Hague in 1850. Later, in 1884, the other part with the representation of the Virgin was bought for the museum.

Rogier van der Weyden, *St Luke Drawing the Virgin.* Oil on canvas (transferred from panel). 102.5 x 108.5 cm

Jan Provost. *The Virgin Mary in Glory.* 1524.
Oil on canvas. 203 x 151 cm

HUGO VAN DER GOES
Circa 1444–1482

Hugo van der Goes was one of major Netherlandish artists. The Hermitage owns two works ascribed to this master. In the altar triptych devoted to Christ's birth the artist creates the beautiful world glistening with gold,

JAN PROVOST
Circa 1456–1529

The *Virgin Mary in Glory* is one of the best altarpieces by Jan Provost. The Virgin stands on a half-moon, surrounded by a golden aureole. In the clouds above are God the Father and God the Holy Ghost. The angels are playing music to glorify Mary as the Mother of God and the young Christ (the glorification of Christ through music and singing derives from the Psalms, in which King David called on all to praise the Lord). In the foreground are prophets and sybils predicting the coming of Christ, the psalmist David, playing his harp, and the Ancient Roman emperor Augustus, who had a vision of the Virgin and Child which was explained to him by the Tiburtine Sibyl.

saturated with bright blue, red and green colour patches, and permeated with a naive and pure faith, which produces a truly indelible impression that only 15th-century Netherlandish artists succeeded to attain in their paintings.

Hugo van der Goes (?). *The Adoration of the Magi.* 1470s. Central part of the triptych of the same name. Oil on canvas. 96.3 x 77.5 cm

NETHERLANDISH SCULPTURE: 16TH CENTURY

The Hermitage has a small collection of Netherlandish statuary, mainly fashioned of wood, dating from the 15th – early 16th centuries. Sculpture was a most popular art form in mediaeval Europe.

It was a major element in the decoration of exteriors and interiors of majestic Christian cathedrals; its role in the life of mediaeval society was far more important. Numerous reliefs depict Bible scenes and episodes from saints' lives. People were able to "read" these reliefs as if they were a book, which made them a sort of "Bible for the poor."

Anonymous Netherlandish masters of the 16th century.
St Jacob. Late 15th – early 16th centuries. Wood. Height 37 cm

Anonymous Netherlandish masters of the 16th century.
St Christopher. Early 16th century. Wood. Height 41 cm

JEAN BELLEGAMBE
Circa 1470–1534

He worked in the lands neighbouring France. Many of his works were commissioned by the celebrated church leader Guillaume of Brussels. He is depicted in the same panel where the Virgin and Archangel are represented, instead of being portrayed on one of the side wings, which had never been done before. The renunciation of the church canons is typical of Renaissance art.

Jean Bellegambe. *The Annunciation.* Triptych. Oil on canvas (transferred from panel).
109.5 x 80 cm (central part), 103 x 33 cm (side wings)

Lucas van Leyden. *The Healing of the Blind Man of Jericho.* 1531. Triptych. Oil on canvas (transferred from panel). 115.5 x 150.5 cm (central part), 89 x 33.5 cm (side wings)

LUCAS VAN LEYDEN
1495/1494 –1533

It is one of the most remarkable works by Lucas van Leyden. The triptych has little in common with religious compositions of the previous period. It is neither pervaded with a deep pious mood nor has a majestic atmosphere. The painting was perhaps intended for the Leyden military hospital rather than for a cathedral altar and so the artist focuses on the moralizing, edifying aspect of the Gospel subject. On the side wings of the triptych the artist placed, instead of traditional images of saints, distinctly secular figures of a warrior and a girl demonstrating coats-of-arms of the commissioners – the Leyden burgher Jacob Floriszon van Monfort and his wife.

MASTER OF THE FEMALE HALF-LENGTHS
Active in the 1530s – 1540s

The painting combines national tradition and the influence of the Italian Renaissance. The still life contains a profound symbolic message: grapes are a traditional attribute of Christ, an emblem of redeeming sacrifice as well as a symbol of the Christian faith and of Holy Communion; cherries hint at the opportunity for the righteous to gain heavenly Paradise in exchange for the earthly Eden which was lost through Original Sin and the Fall of Adam and Eve. Together the grapes and the cherries symbolise the death and resurrection of Jesus Christ.

Master of the Female Half-Lengths.
The Virgin and Child. First half of the 16th century. Oil on panel. 53.2 x 42.4 cm

Master of the Female Half-Lengths. Active in the 1530s –
1540s. *Musicians.* Oil on panel. 53 x 37.5 cm

The technique used by the artist
who depicted large figures half the
complete length, down to the knee
or waist, has been the cause for his
conventional name. The Hermitage
painting manifests the tastes of
the aristocratic milieu which were
formed under the influence of
Italian Renaissance courts and
widespread all over Europe.

Marinus van Roemerswaele.
Tax-Collectors (?). Oil on canvas (transferred
from panel). 84 x 60 cm

MARINUS VAN ROEMERSWAELE
Circa 1490 – circa 1567

The first half of the 16th century
witnessed the appearance in Netherlandish art of new, absolutely realistic
characters which played an important
part in society: bankers, usurers and
money-changers. The most characteristic work representing this kind of
painting is the Hermitage's canvas by
Marinus van Roemerswaele. Tax-collectors did not enjoy great respect in
Netherlandish society and therefore
Roemerswaele's sitters, rendered in
a dry naturalistic manner, with the
attributes of their profession, look
almost as threatening, grotesque
characters.

Dirck Jacobsz. *Group Portrait of the Amsterdam Shooting Corporation.* 1532. Oil on canvas (transferred from panel). 115 x 160 cm

DIRCK JACOBSZ
Circa 1497–1567

A place apart in 16th-century art is held by group portraits which would become very popular in the following century in the Dutch and Flemish schools.

Such portraits, seldom found outside the Netherlands, were mostly commissioned for Town Halls where they are displayed even nowadays. The Hermitage piece by Jacobsz is an early specimen of this form of painting.

Frans Pourbus I. *Portrait of a Man.* Oil on panel. 87 x 78 cm

FRANS POURBUS I
1545–1581

A prominent portrait painter, Pourbus revived the national school of portrait. His Hermitage work combines monumental forms and a tendency to show the restraint and noble dignity of his model, betraying Titian's influence, with the characteristically Netherlandish meticulous rendering of the sitter's individual features.

ABEL GRIMMER
Circa 1570 – before 1619

The Hermitage work by Grimmer is supposed to be one of the four paintings on the theme of seasons. It came from the Yusupovs' palace on the Moyka; the palace catalogue mentions it as *December*. It has a twin painting – *October* (today in the Pushkin Museum of Fine Arts in Moscow).

Abel Grimmer. *Winter Landscape.* Circa 1596. Oil on panel. Diameter 27.8 cm

GIJSDRECHT LIJTENS
1586 – after 1643

Some researches identify the author of this painting, known as the Master of Winter Landscapes, with the Antwerp painter Gijsbrecht Lijtens. In the *Winter Landscape with Wood-Cutters* the artist conveys the interrelationships of light, colour and air medium – the feature that would become a specific quality of Dutch painting.

Gijsbrecht Lijtens. *Winter Landscape with Wood-Cutters.* First quarter of the 17th century. Oil on panel. 71.5 x 89 cm

Pieter Brueghel II. *The Adoration of the Magi.* Oil on canvas (transferred from panel). 36 x 56 cm

PIETER BRUEGHEL II
Circa 1564–1638

The Hermitage works by Pieter Brueghel II give some notion of the oeuvre of his father, the celebrated Netherlandish painter Pieter Brueghel I who had been active in the first half of the 16th century. The son often made copies of his father's compositions.

JAN BRUEGHEL I (VELVET)
1568–1625

Jan Brueghel I, the second son of Pieter Brueghel I, was nicknamed the Velvet Brueghel. He received this nickname largely for his predilection for costly clothes, but another reason was a special velvety quality and softness of his artistic manner. The artist stood on the threshold of innovative discoveries in the field of landscape painting in the 17th century. His harmonious and beautiful art, which covers the turn of the two centuries, completed the great age of the Netherlandish Renaissance.

Jan Brueghel I (Velvet). *Edge of the Forest (The Flight into Egypt).* Oil on copperplate. 25 x 36 cm

German Art: 15th – 20th Centuries

SECOND FLOOR: ROOMS 255–257

The exhibition of German art dating from the 15th – 20th centuries is displayed in the Peter I Gallery, on the second floor of the Small Hermitage. The collection of 15th – 17th-century art is relatively small and does not show a great variance yet it boasts real masterpieces including four works by the outstanding German Renaissance artist Lucas Cranach the Elder. The German artists of the Renaissance attained particular success in the field of portraiture, a notable example of which in the Hermitage is the *Portrait of a Young Man* by Ambrosius Holbein. In the 17th century the flourishing of arts inspired by the Reformation was followed by a crisis when many German artists left for the Netherlands and in the 1630s and later for Holland. This period is represented in the collection by the still lifes of Christopher Paudiss and Georg Flegel.

The Hermitage has a fine collection of pictures by the celebrated 17th-century artist Anton Raphael Mengs who belonged to Neoclassicism as well as by his contemporaries. The Hermitage has a large collection of German applied art that dates from the 16th and 17th centuries.

The Hermitage collection of 19th- and early 20th-century German painting, though relatively small, is considered the best outside Germany. It has works by the adherents of the so-called Nazarene school active in Rome and the painters of the Dusseldorf school and a beautiful assemblage of paintings by the eminent Romantic artist Caspar David Friedrich, known and recognized all over the world. The Hermitage owes Friedrich's works to the Romantic Russian poet Vasily Zhukovsky who has greatly contributed to the better representation of 19th-century German art in the Imperial collection. The German art of the 20th century is exemplified by the Expressionists, close to the Avant-garde movement of the 1910s, first of all by the great master of the 20th century Wassily Kandinsky.

.

Exhibition of German Art:
◀ **15th – 20th Centuries.**
Peter I Gallery

Anonymous artist of the Northern German school. Early 15th century. *Christ at the Last Judgement with the Virgin Mary and St John the Baptist.* Tempera on panel. 46.5 x 70 cm

White lilies rising from the mouth of Jesus symbolize both mercy to the righteous and the sword punishing sinners. Behind Jesus are angels with instruments of passion, by his sides the Virgin and St John the Baptist who intercede for the human race. The painting graced the Town Hall of Elbing and was meant to serve as a model for the earthly judges.

Lucas Cranach the Elder. *Venus and Cupid.* 1509.
Oil on canvas (transferred from panel). 213 x 102 cm

Lucas Cranach the Elder. *The Virgin and Child under an Apple Tree.* 1528. Oil on canvas (transferred from panel). 87 x 59 cm

LUCAS CRANACH THE ELDER
1472–1553

Venus and Cupid is the earliest of Cranach's works based on this subject. It is generally believed that the Hermitage painting was the first ever attempt in Northern Europe to represent the goddess of love and beauty naked. During the Reformation period the image of Venus was associated with the sin of sensuality as it is emphasized by the Latin inscription in the upper part of the work: "Study with all your might to resist the voluptuous Cupid / Lest blind Love master your captive heart." Cranach's female characters, whether his contemporaries or biblical or mythological images, are always somewhat mysterious and restrained. A typical example of such a mysterious German beauty is the Hermitage's *Portrait of a Woman*.

Lucas Cranach the Elder. *Portrait of a Woman.* 1526. Oil on panel. 88.5 x 58.5 cm

Ambrosius Holbein. *Portrait of a Young Man.* 1518.
Tempera and oil on panel. 44 x 32.5 cm

AMBROSIUS HOLBEIN
Circa 1495 — circa 1519

This talented painter was the elder brother of Hans Holbein the Younger, an outstanding master of the German Renaissance. He died at the age of twenty-four and left few works that are a great rarity even in German collections. The portrait of a young man was evidently created at Basle that in the early 16th century was considered a major centre of Humanism in Germany and had close ties with Italy.

Bartholomaus Bruyn I. *Portrait of a Lady and Her Daughter.* Late 1530s — early 1540s. Oil on canvas (transferred from panel). 75.5 x 46 cm

BARTHOLOMAUS BRUYN I
1493—1555

A talented Renaissance artist, Bruyn from Cologne was at his best in portrait painting. He worked on numerous commissions from local burghers. The Hermitage twin portraits of a man and woman with children are typical family portraits, fashion for which came to Germany from the Netherlands.

Hans von Aachen. *The Allegory of Peace, Art and Abundance.* 1602. Oil on canvas. 197 x 142 cm

ADAM ELSHEIMER
1578–1610

The oeuvre of this artist is marked by interest in light effects. The moonlight is most important for his *St Christopher*. It renders a some-what mystical, elevated character to Elsheimer's interpretation of the story of a pagan strong man who met Christ the Child and was con-verted to Christianity.

Cabinet on a stand. Late 16th – early 17th centuries. Tyrol. Pine and ash woods; carving and intarsia

This cabinet clearly belongs to the Baroque style. Such motifs as the perspective view of a portal, with a well or fountain in the foreground, round balconies in the lateral compositions and the architectural view in the background were all bor-rowed from the engravings by the Netherlandish orna-mental painter Hans Vredeman de Vries. Some pieces use texture to im-itate marble, a feature typical of the work of Tyrolean masters from the end of the 16th century.

HANS VON AACHEN
1552–1615

Hans von Aachen was a typical representative of the unusual, very cosmopolitan school of painting which developed in Prague at the turn of the 16th and 17th centuries at the court of Emperor Rudolf II. The symbolism of the theme (*Allegory of Peace, Art and Abundance*) was intended to praise the emperor's peaceful policies, which led to prosperity.

Adam Elsheimer. *St Christopher.* Oil on copperplate. 22.5 x 17.5 cm

Daniel Schultz. *Family Portrait.* 1664. Oil on canvas. 166 x 231 cm

DANIEL SHULTZ
1615–1683

Daniel Schultz, a talented German artist, made his career outside his native country. Perhaps the artist's most important work, this family portrait, was painted in Gdansk.

In turning to official portraiture, he retained all the characteristics of the type but majesty and formality here give way to the great realism of the scene of celebration that has been arranged in honour of the elder son's becoming a royal falconer.

JURGEN OVENS
1623–1679

Ovens created historical paintings and portraits. He was closely associated with the Dutch school. He mastered artistic skills at the workshop of Rembrandt from whom he borrowed the range of warm brown tones, expressive chiaroscuro effects and interest in portraiture.

Jurgen Ovens. *Self-Portrait of the Artist at the Easel.* Oil on canvas. 125 x 95 cm

Christopher Paudiss. *Still Life.* 1660. Oil on canvas (transferred from panel). 62 x 46.5 cm

CHRISTOPHER PAUDISS
Circa 1625–1666

Paudiss was a gifted artist who studied at Rembrandt's workshop in the 1640s. This still life is done in the lyrical Naturalist tradition of the 17th-century Dutch school. The objects are shown with such naturalness and simplicity that is rare even in this school. The main element of Paudiss's work is the light that fills the entire space of the painting.

ANGELICA KAUFFMAN
1741–1807

German by origin, Kauffman made her artistic career in Italy and Britain. She gained fame for her sentimental compositions based on subjects from Classical Antiquity and modern literature. In this painting she depicts the moment at which Octavia, sister of the Emperor Augustus, loses consciousness as she listens to Virgil reading his verses and recalls the early death of her son.

Angelica Kauffman. *Virgil Reading the "Aeneid" to Augustus and Octavia.* 1788. Oil on canvas. 123 x 159 cm

Anton Raffael Mengs. *Self-Portrait.* Circa 1775. Oil on panel. 102 x 77 cm

ANTON RAFFAEL MENGS
1728–1779

Mengs was one of the founders of Neoclassicism, a movement born in the second half of the 18th century in Europe which demonstrated great reverence for the heritage of Antiquity. The monumental painting *Perseus and Andromeda* is a programmatic Neoclassical work. Its story is full of adventures. Done in Italy, it was sent to the commissioner in England on board the ship which was captured by pirates. In the port of Cadiz the pirates sold the painting to some unknown person and later it found its way to the French marine minister and, finally, was acquired for the collection of Catherine II.

Anton Raffael Mengs. *Perseus and Andromeda.* 1777. Oil on canvas. 227 x 153.5 cm

HEINRICH FUGER
1751–1818

An Austrian painter and engraver who also produced miniatures, Fuger worked in Vienne, lived in Rome and Naples. He painted frescos and pictures on the subjects from ancient mythology and history and also created quite a number of portraits. Fuger offers a somewhat romantic interpretation of the personality of Prince Nikolai Yusupov, Russian diplomat and art lover who selected in Rome works for Catherine II's collection.

Heinrich Fuger. *Portrait of Prince Nikolai Yusupov.* 1783. Oil on canvas. 112 x 67 cm

Clock. 18th century. Meissen. Porcelain and bronze; gilding and overglaze painting. 52 x 55 cm

The Meissen Factory, established in 1710, earned European renown when it was supervised by Joachim Kendler. His designs were used to produce beautiful vases, grand services, chandeliers and decorative statuettes intended for the embellishment of clocks, mirrors and caskets. His manner that brought to life numerous imitators is marked by a special dynamism and elaborate rhythms typical of the "gallant" Rococo style.

Caspar David Friedrich. *Riesengebirge (Giant Mountains).* 1818–20. Oil on canvas. 71 x 56 cm

Caspar David Friedrich. *On a Sailing Boat.* 1818–20. Oil on canvas. 71 x 56 cm

CASPAR DAVID FRIEDRICH
1774–1840

On a Sailing Boat is a very rare romanticized reflection of the real event. It was created soon after Friedrich's wedding travel with his young wife Caroline to Rugen Island. It symbolizes the joint sailing of the two lovers across the "sea of life," their mutual aspiration to lofty ideals.

CARL FRIEDRICH LESSING
1808–1880

Royal Couple Mourning for Their Dead Daughter is the first large-scale painting by the Dusseldorf artist. It was exhibited in Berlin in 1830 and inspired admiration in the general public. A real-life episode was interpreted by the Romantic artist in the mediaeval "terms" as an event from the distant past.

Carl Friedrich Lessing. *Royal Couple Mourning for Their Dead Daughter.* 1830. Oil on canvas. 215 x 193 cm

Friedrich Johann Overbeck. *The Triumph of Religion in the Arts.* 1839–1843.
Author's replica. Oil on canvas. 145 x 146 cm

FRIEDRICH JOHANN OVERBECK
1789–1869

Overbeck was a founder of the Nazarene school. The movement's ideological leader, he strove to revive a monumental religious style in art. His clear-cut composition displays harmony and a sincere and elevated faith in God, the characteristics which, according to Overbeck, only the Early Renaissance artists had attained.

ANSELM FEUERBACH
1829–1880

Nephew of the famous philosopher, he belonged to the so-called "Italian" Germans, as he lived most of his life in Rome and Venice. In their subject matter his paintings are closer to Romantic art: they are based on Oriental motifs, subjects from the life and poetry of Dante, Petrarch, Ariosto etc. His *Self-Portrait* is also done in the Romantic vein. Shown in profile, the artist is somewhat separated from the crowd.

Anselm Feuerbach. *Self-Portrait.*
Oil on canvas. 92 x 73 cm

Franz von Stuck. *Fighting for a Woman*. 1905. Oil on panel. 90 x 17 cm

FRANZ VON STUCK
1863–1928

Franz von Stuck was a central figure in German artistic life in the late 19th century, a foremost Symbolist artist and co-founder of the Munich Secession. His *Fighting for a Woman* was inspired by Friedrich Nietzsche's works. Showing the power of natural instincts, Stuck depicted exaggeratedly brutal figures, made visible in the darkness with the help of uneven light contrasted by gloomy shadows.

WASSILY KANDINSKY
1866–1944

A leading 20th-century artist, Kandinsky was born in Russia. In 1911 he founded the influential Munich group Der Blaue Reiter ("The Blue Rider") which propagated Avant-garde art. His four Hermitage works date from the Munich and early Moscow periods of his career. One of them is the well-known abstract *Composition V*.

Wassily Kandinsky. *Composition V*. 1913. Oil on canvas. 194 x 294 cm

Heinrich Ehmsen. *Execution by Firing Squad (Red Jacket).* 1919. Oil on canvas. 109.3 x 135 cm

HEINRICH EHMSEN
1886–1964

This German artist was influenced by Die Brucke ("The Bridge") group of Expressionists critical of the abnormalities of the modern civilization. Representative of the radical left-wing, he painted this work under the impression made on him by the massacre of the Bavarian Republic leaders.

HEINRICH CAMPEDONK
1889–1957

This German artist was member of the Der Blaue Reiter ("The Blue Rider") group. Struck by World War I's events, he gave preference to the world of idealized images and fantasy. *Man and Beasts amidst Nature* is a typical work of Campedonk who was fond of old stained-glass panels.

Heinrich Campedonk. *Man and Beasts amidst Nature.* 1920s. Oil on canvas. 95 x 65.5 cm

The Old Hermitage

History and Architecture

The Old, or Large, Hermitage was built to a design by Yury Velten in 1770–1787 for the rapidly growing collections of Catherine the Great which the Small Hermitage failed to accommodate. The second Hermitage structure put up alongside the Palace Embankment was originally called "the structure in line with the Hermitage." It changed its name only in the middle of the 19th century, when the New Hermitage was attached to it on the side of Bolshaya Milionnaya Street. Then it began to be named the Old Hermitage

The architectural history of the building, closely interwoven with the development of the entire complex of the Imperial residence, can be divided into two periods. The first one encompasses the late 18th and early 19th centuries. The second period covers the middle of the 19th century when the interiors were redesigned and refurnished.

At first Velten erected a small block linking it by a passage to the Small Hermitage. Then Catherine the Great ordered him to extend it down to the corner of the Palace Embankment and Winter Canal. Soon after putting up the Hermitage Theatre on the opposite bank of the canal, Velten spanned the Winter Canal with an arched passageway thus linking the whole architectural ensemble of the Imperial residence facing the Neva. The architect paid a special attention to the decor of the second-floor interiors of the Old Hermitage that formed the Neva Suite of state rooms. The empress passed this suite during her official "grand entrees" after performances in the Hermitage Theatre. The ceremony of passing through the rooms adorned with paintings of the Italian, Spanish and Dutch schools, glyptic and numismatic collections usually ended in the Northern Pavilion of the Small Hermitage with a large assembly attended by up to 300 guests.

Council Staircase

In the early 1850s, in connection with the construction of a special museum building, the New Hermitage, and the transfer to it of the larger part of the collections, the designation and decor of the interiors of the Old Hermitage were altered. Since the lower storey of the building was to accommodate the State Council and the Cabinet of Ministers of the Russian Empire, the architect Andrei Stakenschneider created on the place of the Oval Hall, where famous Voltaire's library had been kept in Catherine's reign, the State (later Council) Staircase linking the rooms of the State Council with the Small Hermitage and the Winter Palace. Emperor Nicholas I commissioned Stakenschneider to redecorate the Old Hermitage suite of state rooms for the living quarters of Tsesarevich Nicholas Alexandrovich. The architect left the layout of the rooms unaltered, yet with a subtle taste and creative imagination, he redecorated them, achieving consummate perfection in combining elements of diverse historical styles and a variety of art forms and materials.

Towards the end of the 1850s the decoration of the new halls and rooms was completed. The terminally ill heir, however, died at Nice and never saw his apartments. Now this architectural setting created by Stakenschneider is used for the display of one of the most celebrated Hermitage's collections – Italian art of the Renaissance.

Railings of the Council Staircase

The Council Entrance

The Council Entrance leading to the rooms on the first floor of the Old Hermitage intended for the State Council's meetings was opened in 1828. Ascending the elegant white marble staircase, also known as the Council Staircase, the visitor comes onto the landing of the second floor skirted with slender columns of white Carrara marble. The ceiling painted by the French 18th-century artist Gabriel Francois Doyen is the only part of decor retained by Stakenschneider from the Oval Hall. The allegorical painting reminds the viewer that the Hermitage had once belonged to the "Russian Minerva," as Catherine the Great, a patroness of sciences, arts and crafts, was sometimes called.

The Leonardo da Vinci Room

The former main state "hall with two windows" and other rooms of the Old Hermitage facing the Neva were designed in the early 19th century by Giacomo Quarenghi. The hall housed the collection of Italian painters of the 15th to 18th centuries and was known as the Italian Hall. Stakenschneider transformed the hall into a

Flight of stairs of the Council Staircase

Proto-Renaissance Room. Exhibition of Italian Art: 13th – 14th Centuries

Leonardo da Vinci Room

luxurious palatial interior striking by a variety of its decor in rare costly materials. Of special beauty are the red-green columns of band Kushkul jasper set on fireplaces of white Carrara marble. The fireplaces are embellished with lapis lazuli and mosaic panels. The unique doors of the hall fashioned of ebony are decorated with an ornament imitating the Boulle technique – a combination of tortoise-shell and gilded copper. The painted panels by Alessandro Padovanino had been in this interior before the reconstruction. Stakenschneider added to them several smaller panels by Fyodor Bruni. Over the doors are medallions with the portraits of Field Marshals Suvorov, Rumyantsev, Paskevich and Kutuzov. Nowadays two masterpieces, the *Benois Madonna* and the *Litta Madonna* by Leonardo da Vinci, are displayed in this magnificent room which is named after this great Italian artist.

Italian Art: 14th – 16th Centuries
SECOND FLOOR: ROOMS 207–223

The Old Hermitage houses the Italian Renaissance collection, one of most celebrated assemblages of the museum. Its considerable part, including *Judith* by Giorgione, Raphael's *Holy Family* and *Danae* by Titian, was acquired in the reign of Catherine II. In the 19th century the Hermitage was enriched with some other works by Titian, Leonardo da Vinci's *Litta Madonna* and the *Conestabile Madonna* by Raphael. In the early 20th century a number of first-rate paintings from the 14th and 15th centuries joined the museum collection, among them *Madonna* from the *Annunciation* diptych by Simone Martini and another work by Leonardo – the *Benois Madonna* (*Madonna with a Flower*). After the Revolution of 1917 the Hermitage received Italian paintings from nationalized private and museum collections. Nevertheless, in the 1920s and 1930s it lost such world-famous masterpieces as *Venus with a Mirror* by Titian, Raphael's *St George* and *Alba Madonna* and Sandro Botticelli's *Adoration of the Magi* sold to foreign countries by the Soviet government.

Chronologically the Italian Renaissance divides into two unequal phases. The early period covers the 15th century (it is known as the Quattrocento). The second period is the High Renaissance (from the late 15th century to the 1530s). In Venice it continued till the late 16th century. The Early Renaissance, or Qattrocento, was preceded by a phase which lasted more than a century – the so-called Proto-Renaissance. It is with a rather small Proto-Renaissance collection that the Hermitage displays of Italian art start. The most famous works in the Hermitage are paintings by the geniuses of the High Renaissance – Leonardo da Vinci and Raphael (exhibited in the Old Hermitage), as well as by Titian and Michelangelo (the latter is represented by a single sculpture) (exhibited in the New Hermitage). Together with masterworks of Italian Renaissance painters and sculptors, the Old Hermitage rooms hold splendid specimens of applied art from the period which was marked by the unrivalled achievements in all art forms. These are examples of metalwork, Venetian glass, tapestries and embroideries that once abundantly decorated gorgeous Italian palazzos.

Proto-Renaissance Room.
◀ **Exhibition of Italian Art:**
13th – 14th Centuries

SIMONE MARTINI
Circa 1284–1344

The earliest Renaissance period is also called Proto-Renaissance and covers the late 13th and 14th centuries. Works by artists of this period, dubbed "primitives" in the 18th and 19th centuries, still betray traditions of European Gothic art and Byzantine icon-painting – the two powerful elements of mediaeval art. The recognized masterpiece of the Hermitage collection dating from the Proto-Renaissance period is the right wing of the *Annunciation* diptych painted by great Martini, a renowned artist born in Sienna. Nobody knows when the wings of the diptych were separated. The left-hand wing showing the Archangel Gabriel is now at the National Gallery in Washington.

Simone Martini. *Madonna* from the *Annunciation*. Circa 1340–44, Tempera on panel. 30.5 x 21.5 cm

Niccolo di Pietro Gerini. *The Crucifixion with the Virgin and St John*. Between 1390 and 1395. Tempera on panel. 85.5 x 52.7 cm

NICCOLO DI PIETRO GERINI
Mentioned in 1368–1415

The *Crucifixion with the Virgin and St John* was listed in the manuscript catalogue of the Count Pavel Stroganov collection as a work by of one of Giotto's followers. The tradition of mediaeval painting is still strongly felt in the conventional treatment of the figures depicted on a flat golden background and in the symmetry and balance of the composition. The Latin letters I.N.R.I. over the Crucifix denote the name and guilt of the executed person – *Iesus Nasarenus Rex Iudaeorum* (Jesus of Nazareth, King of the Jews). The gilded Gothic frame bears the inscription: *PATER. NOSTER. QVIES.INCIELIS.SANTIFI* (Lat.: Our Father Who art in Heavens).

Fra Beato Angelico da Fiesole. *Madonna and Child with Sts Dominic and Thomas Aquinas.* Between 1424 and 1430. Tempera on plaster. 196 x 187 cm

FRA BEATO ANGELICO DA FIESOLE
Circa 1400–1455

Fra Beato Angelico da Fiesole. *Madonna and Child with Angels.* Circa 1425. Tempera on panel. 80 x 51 cm

Fra Beato Angelico da Fiesole was one of the most poetic and elevated artists of the Early Renaissance. He took monastic vows and spent his entire life in endless toil, painting holy images on the walls of monasteries near Florence. His rare for museum collections fresco *Madonna and Child with Sts Dominic and Thomas Aquinas* was done for the refectory of the

Monastery of St Dominic at Fiesole in the 1420s. In the second half of the 19th century the monastery was closed, the valuable murals cut out and sold. The fresco with the Madonna became the property of two Florentine painters from whom it was acquired for the Imperial Hermitage in 1883.

ANTONIO ROSSELINO
1427–1479

The assemblage of sculpture in the Old Hermitage rooms is not very large. Nevertheless some of its specimens can rival in their mastery best paintings from the period. The marble relief *Madonna and Child* by the foremost Quattrocento master Antonio Rosselino, who was dubbed by his contemporaries "Raphael of sculpture," is considered one of the best examples of Renaissance plastic art.

Antonio Rosselino. *Madonna and Child.* Mid-15th century. Marble. 67 x 54 cm

Giovanni della Robbia. *The Nativity.* Early 16th century. Majolica. 262 x 167 cm

GIOVANNI DELLA ROBBIA
1469 – circa 1529

Giovanni della Robbia was member of the famous Florentine dynasty of pottery artists active in the 15th – early 16th centuries. This family invented polychrome majolica, painted and fired earthenware covered with coloured glazing. The large-scale *Nativity* done by Giovanni della Robbia came to the Hermitage in the mid-1880s from the collection of the Russian diplomat Alexander Basilewski.

BERNARDINO FUNGAI
1460–1516

The Hermitage painting by Bernardino Fungai done on the *cassone* board is one of most noteworthy of his works. The subject from Antiquity is shown here as a colourful picturesque scene in which Roman general Scipio Africanus, his companions (horsemen and foot soldiers) and other characters are wearing Renaissance costumes. The Toscana landscape in the background is meticulously rendered.

Bernardino Fungai. *The Magnanimity of Scipio Africanus.* Oil on panel. 62 x 166 cm

SANDRO BOTTICELLI (ALESSANDRO DA MARIANO DI VANNI DI AMEDEO FILIPEPI)
1445–1510

This remarkable Renaissance artist is represented in the Hermitage collection by twin paintings – *St Dominic* and *St Jerome*. The first piece shows St Dominic at the moment of vision. The saint sees Jesus Christ with cherubim and angels blowing trumpets and announcing the coming of the Doomsday. Both paintings date from the artist's late period when the actual ruler of Florence was Savonarola, a monk and fanatic religious reformer, whose ideas had a great impact on Botticelli.

Sandro Botticelli. *St Dominic.* Between 1498 and 1505. Tempera on canvas. 44.5 x 26 cm

FILIPPINO LIPPI
Circa 1457–1504

Son of the celebrated artist Fra Filippo Lippi, he started his career at the workshop of Botticelli. In the 1480s he ceased using Florentine linear forms characteristic of his teacher. Under the influence of Leonardo da Vinci he strove to render the light and atmosphere effects, which is to be seen in his tondo (circular painting) – the *Adoration of the Infant Christ.*

Filippino Lippi. *The Adoration of the Infant Christ.* Mid-1480s. Oil on copperplate (transferred from panel). Diameter 53 cm

GIORGIONE (GIORGIO DA CASTELFRANCO)
Circa 1478–1510

This outstanding Venetian artist was one of those who brought the High Renaissance to Venice. His biography has many vague moments to this day: he never signed his works and no more than ten paintings are definitely ascribed to him today, although some scholars increase this number to several dozens. The date of Giorgione's birth is also unknown – the only available fact is that he died in his early thirties during the epidemic of plague in 1510. The Hermitage owns one of Giorgione's masterpieces – his *Judith*.

This biblical heroine who had saved her native city Bethulia attacked by the Assyrian troops was very pop-

Giorgione. *Madonna and Child.* Circa 1503. Oil on canvas. 44 x 36.5 cm

ular in Italian Renaissance painting. Judith secretly penetrated to the enemy's camp and charmed the army leader by her beauty. After a feast, during the night, she decapitated Holofernes. The poetic charming image of the girl, the coolness of the morning landscape enhance the impression of calm contemplation, not distorted by the grimace of death on Holofernes' face.

The second Hermitage's painting by Giorgione is the more intimate *Madonna and Child.* It depicts Mary carefully holding the head of the Child as he falls to sleep. The warm colouring creates the sense of evening light. We look upon the scene from a high point of view, but for all the grand scale of the painting's subject it looks lyrical. Since the late 15th century Renaissance masters were increasingly departing from tradition in their depictions of the Virgin. Instead of placing her on a throne, surrounded by saints, they might show her in a landscape. Such works were often small, intended for private chapels.

Giorgione. *Judith.* Early 1500s. Oil on canvas (transferred from panel). 144 x 68 cm

PIETRO PERUGINO (PIETRO VANNUCCI)
Circa 1445/48–1523

Perugino was a leading Quattro-cento artist and representative of the Umbrian school. Raphael was among his pupils. His compositions are clear and well devised, marked by harmony and balance. His characters are full of lyricism. They seem calm, yet concentrated and deep in their thoughts.

Pietro Perugino. *Portrait of a Young Man.* Circa 1500. Oil on canvas. 40.5 x 25.5 cm

LORENZO COSTA
Circa 1460–1535

The painting style of the artist, born in Ferrara, developed in Bologna, to which he moved at the age of 23. From the early 16th century Bolognese painting was strongly influenced by Raphael and this portrait of an unknown lady was, until the early 20th century, attributed to the great master from Urbino himself.

The simple and laconic composition of this portrait is typical of the late 15th and early 16th centuries. Its dark background and restrained colouring, the somewhat flat rendering of the torso and shoulders, all force the viewer to concentrate on the sitter's face. The barely perceptible smile and lively look in her large intelligent eyes suggest an energetic and cheerful personality.

Lorenzo Costa (?). *Portrait of a Lady.* Between 1500 and 1506. Oil on canvas. 57 x 44 cm

Leonardo da Vinci. *Madonna with a Flower (Benois Madonna).*
1478. Oil on canvas (transferred from panel). 49.5 x 31.5 cm

LEONARDO DA VINCI
1452–1519

The painted legacy of Leonardo is not extensive. It numbers twelve to fourteen works signed by the artist, to which the two magnificent *Madonnas*

Leonardo da Vinci. *Madonna and Child (Litta Madonna).* 1470 – circa 1490/91. Tempera on canvas (transferred from panel). 42 x 33 cm

possessed by the Hermitage belong. The *Madonna with a Flower*, or *Benois Madonna* (owned by the family of the architect Leonty Benois before it came to the Hermitage), is executed in oil, the medium which was unusual for that period. Leonardo depicts the Madonna as a young Florentine woman wearing a fashionable dress and playing with her child. These realistic elements, however, are combined with traditional symbolism: shown over the heads of the Madonna and the Child are thin golden haloes; the baby strives to catch the four-petal flower that alludes to the form of the Cross.

For the other Hermitage representation of the Madonna the painter used the medium of tempera, traditional for Italy. Later the picture came to be also known as the *Litta Madonna* after the name of its first owner – the Milanese Count Antoine Litta. The image of the Madonna typifies the ideal of beauty of the High Renaissance in which physical perfection is inseparable from spiritual elevation.

Jacopo Palma. *Portrait of a Man.*
Circa 1512–13. Oil on canvas (transferred
from panel). 93.5 x 72 cm

CORREGIO (ANTONIO ALLEGRI)
1489/94–1534

Antonio Allegri was called Correggio
after his native city. This canvas ranks
among the best works in the Hermitage
collection of Italian paintings. The sitter
is shown wearing a mourning dress.
Her brown robe and belt evidence
that she belongs to the Franciscan
Order. The laurel wreath on her head
is a symbol of poetry and hints at her
poetic talents. The tree trunk wound
around with ivy symbolizes matrimonial
faithfulness and eternal love.

Francesco Melzi. *Portrait of a Woman
(Flora).* Circa 1520. Oil on canvas. 76 x 63 cm

JACOPO PALMA
(JACOPO NEGRETTI)
1480–1528

Palma was an illustrious representative of the Venetian school and
follower of Giorgione and Titian. His
Hermitage work is one of the best
examples of portraiture from the
period. The portrayed young man
is marked by genuine aristocratism,
dignity, nobleness and easy manner. The characteristics of the sitter, member of Venetian high society, are emphasized by the refined
colour scheme based on the combination of silvery, yellow and brown
tones.

Corregio. *Portrait of a Lady.* Circa 1519.
Oil on canvas. 103 x 87.5 cm

FRANCESCO MELZI
1493–1570

Francesco Melzi was Leonardo's
favourite pupil. In 1516 the young
Melzi followed the 64-year-old
Leonardo, his teacher and friend, to
France where he faithfully looked
after him until the death of the great
master. *Flora*, or *Columbine* (from
the name of the flower, columbine,
in the model's hand), entered the
Hermitage in 1850 from the collection
of King William II of the Netherlands
as a work by Leonardo da Vinci.
Today it is exactly known that the
painting was executed by Melzi.

Titian (Tiziano Vecellio). *Portrait of a Young Woman.* 1530s. Oil on canvas. 96 x 75 cm

TITIAN (TIZIANO VECELLIO)
1488/90–1576

The work of Titian, Giorgione's pupil and leader of the Venetian school, marked the culmination of the Italian Renaissance. The Venetians revered their compatriot who lived a long life and never ceased to amaze them by his mastery. The Hermitage has eight paintings by Titian. Almost all of them belong to his mature period when his remarkable talent was developed to the utmost. Titian turned to the antique myth of Danae not once, translating into colour his admiration for woman's beauty. The Hermitage painting is one of several versions painted by the artist. The *Repentant Mary Magdalene* painted in the same period is Titian's acknowledged masterpiece. The Hermitage canvas features St Mary at a moment of her passionate agitated prayer. *St Sebastian* was painted by the artist when he was 85. The huge canvas, however, is pervaded with energy and beauty.

Titian (Tiziano Vecellio). *The Repentant Mary Magdalene.* 1560s. Oil on canvas. 119 x 97 cm

Titian (Tiziano Vecellio). *Danae*. Between 1546 and 1553. Oil on canvas. 120 x 187 cm

Titian (Tiziano Vecellio). *St Sebastian*. 1570s. Oil on canvas.
210 x 115.5 cm

Paolo Veronese. *The Adoration of the Magi.* 1570s. Oil on copperplate. 45 x 34.5 cm

Paolo Veronese. *The Pieta.* Between 1576 and 1582. Oil on canvas. 147 x 111.5 cm

PAOLO VERONESE (PAOLO CALIARI)
1528–1588

Born in Verona, Paolo Caliari, dubbed Veronese, settled in Venice in 1555 and soon became one of the most illustrious artists of the Republic. He created numerous multi-figured compositions and brilliant portraits distinguished by splendid colours and a festive atmosphere of celebration. The Hermitage possesses seven works by the master: small sketches and large-scale canvases featuring religious subjects.

Pontormo (Jacopo Carrucci). *Madonna and Child with Sts Joseph and John the Baptist.* Late 1521 – early 1522. Oil on canvas. 120 x 98.5 cm

PONTORMO (JACOPO CARRUCCI)
1494–1557

Pontormo was born and spent all his life in Florence. He was a master of the early Mannerism, a style which moved away from the principles of the High Renaissance with its striving for harmony and lofty beauty. The single work by Pontormo in the Hermitage collection has a monumental composition and decorative colour scale based on colour discords, which enhances the emotional misbalance of the characters depicted in the painting. This is typical of all the works painted by the Mannerists.

Bowl with long stem. Second half of the 16th century. Height 15.5 cm; diameter 13.3 cm
Jug. Last quarter of the 16th century. Venice. Colourless glass; blown into a form and inset with milky threads

Flounce. Mid-17th century. Guipure and linen thread; weaving. Fragment

Lace originated in Italy. Its predecessor was openwork embroidery with geometric patterns stitched upon a more or less open fabric. Venice gave rise to the development of guipure which combined bobbin and needle types of lace.

Glassmaking was born in Venice in the 13th century and reached its acme in the High Renaissance period. To protect the secret techniques of glassmaking the Venetians moved their workshops to the small island of Murano. The name of the island was given to the type of glass produced there. Most exquisite items were made of this glass whose composition was unique. Most popular were items covered with a lacy white pattern (milky glass threads were set into the hot glass body).

The Hermitage Theatre

History and Architecture

The building of the Old Hermitage occupies a place on the Palace Embankment limited from the east by the narrow Winter Canal linking the two rivers – the wide, deep Neva and the small, winding Moyka. On the opposite bank of the Winter Canal stood the Winter Palace of Peter the Great built in the early 18th century, but towards the end of the century it became dilapidated and deserted. In 1783 Catherine the Great ordered Giacomo Quarenghi, her court architect, to erect a new "home" theatre there. A decree about its construction was signed on 6 November 1783, and, two years later, a white-columned edifice linked to the Old Hermitage with an elegant arch in the Venetian style that spanned the Winter Canal was completed. On 16 November 1785, a record was made in the court journal informing that the empress, together with her most august family "...proceeded through the Hermitage to the new theatre and attended a rehearsal of a comic opera." The theatre became the favourite resting place of Catherine II. Usually the entire royal court, the heir's family, diplomats and other invited persons were present at performances. Quarenghi had succeeded in creating a genuine masterpiece of architecture and most perfect palatial building of Russia and Europe. It harmoniously combined the best accomplishments of European theatrical architecture – excellent acoustics, comfortable stage, cosy seats for spectators – with an elegance and a sense of intimacy befitting a domestic Imperial theatre.

Winter Canal

Foyer

The architecture of the auditorium delighted contemporaries and confirmed the designer's opinion that the shape of covered amphitheatre was the most comfortable one. "The seats are not designated to particular persons, no special etiquette is to be observed and everyone can sit where he/she chooses," wrote the architect. The Hermitage Theatre staged operas, comedies and dramas. The empress had an eye on the staging of productions and herself indulged in playwriting. Among the theatre's conductors were such European celebrities as Cimarosa, Galuppi and Paisiello. Best Russian and foreign com-

The Foyer

The Hermitage Theatre begins with a foyer located in the upper part of the arched bridge. The two longitudinal walls of the hall, pierced with windows from top to bottom, create an illusion of an open space over the expanses of the Neva on the one side and over the closed elegant world of the Winter Canal on the other. The foyer acquired its present-day appearance in 1904, after a new redecoration, undertaken by the architect Leonty Benois in imitation of the Rococo style.

The Auditorium

The architect used the ground floor of the former Winter Palace of Peter the Great as a basement and put up on it a majestic auditorium remarkable for its balanced and harmonious proportions. Taking the form of the Ancient Roman theatre as his model, Quarenghi resolved the rows in the shape of an amphitheatre. He adorned the scenic portal and the walls with Corinthian semicolumns and niches and faced them with polychrome artificial marble. He skilfully introduced into the ensemble of the au-

Foyer. Ceiling painting: *The Rape of Europe.* **By Luca Giordano. 17th century. Fragment**

Auditorium

ditorium decorative reliefs and sculpture. The architect himself wrote: "...in the ten niches of the auditorium and proscenium I set up the statues of Apollo and the Nine Muses, while in the squares over the niches I installed the busts and medallions of contemporary theatrical celebrities."

Auditorium. *Allegorical Figure.* **By Concese Albani. 1784. Marble**

panies and orchestras, as well as single singers, gave performances here.

Today plays and concerts are given at the Hermitage Theatre every night and artists from leading St Petersburg, other Russian and world theatres perform on its stage. Like in the 18th century, the audience, seated comfortably on the velvet-covered seats, enjoys the performances. The spectators can "see each other well and when the auditorium is full of people, it is a pleasant sight" as it used to be in the time of Quarenghi who wrote these lines.

Theatre curtain

The Winter Palace of Peter I

History and Architecture

Under the Hermitage Theatre there is a unique memorial exhibition – "The Winter Palace of Peter I." It has been created quite recently. A research of the basements undertaken in the course of the theatre restoration carried out in 1987–89 by the Hermitage specialists unexpectedly revealed authentic architectural fragments of the former Peter's palace (included into the foundation of a later structure from Catherine II's reign). The construction of the Winter Palace of Peter the Great began in 1716 to a design of Johann Mattarnovi and was completed in 1723, shortly before Peter's death, by another architect, Domenico Trezzini.

The rooms of the third and last Winter Palace of Peter the Great survived without any decoration, so it was impossible to find out the purpose of each particular interior. The reconstructed interiors of the Dining Room, Study and Turnery display objects formerly used at the royal court, considered fashionable in Peter's reign and later kept in the Hermitage stocks.

The dinner table is covered with an Oriental carpet; set on it is silverware and a most noteworthy item – an uncorked original bottle of wine (18th century) discovered among the building debris in the cause of restoration works carried out here.

Dining Room

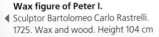

Wax figure of Peter I.
◀ Sculptor Bartolomeo Carlo Rastrelli.
1725. Wax and wood. Height 104 cm

In the courtyard, surviving in a very good state, with the pavement of the Petrine age, stands a carriage made shortly before Peter's death. It is one of the two extant vehicles in Russia made after drawings by the celebrated French sculptor Nicholas Pineau.

Peter the Great died in his Winter Palace in the last days of January 1725. His coffin, together with the coffin of his daughter Natalia, stood for forty days on a special platform in the Cavaliers Room and then was transported across the Neva River (on ice) to the Sts Peter and Paul Cathedral located right opposite the palace on the other bank.

"Small Chambers." Peter's writing desk with a folding flap in the foreground

The Hermitage has a large and varied stock of scientific devices, machinery and instruments associated with the life and activities of Peter the Great. Some noteworthy items from the memorabilia are displayed in the Winter Palace of Peter I. The centerpiece of the exhibition is the so-called Turnery, court workshop of the emperor who was fond of turning. The development of the craft was much contributed to by Andrei Nartov, "court turner" to Emperor Peter, an outstanding Russian engineer who invented dozens of mechanisms and devices and headed the Turnery since 1723. With the help of its turning and copying machines and dies the workshop produced from ivory and different types of wood abundantly ornamented caskets, snuff-boxes, bowls and cups as well as multi-figured compositions. Many of the objects were fashioned personally by the emperor.

State Courtyard

Now the exhibition of the palace includes the posthumous wax effigy of the tsar produced by Bartolomeo Carlo Rastrelli on the order of Catherine II. Plaster casts from Peter's face, hands and feet were made by the sculptor soon after the emperor's death. The completed work was an exact copy of his outward appearance. All his clothes are authentic (he was 2.4 m tall).

Thus two most significant historical ages covered by the glory of the two great emperors, Peter I and Catherine II, have met in the Hermitage Theatre built in the second half of the 18th century.

Turnery

Grigory Musikiysky. Miniature painting: *Family Portrait of Peter I. 1716–17*

Anonymous artist. *Portrait of the Heir Apparent Peter Petrovich* (1715–19)

Anonymous artist. *Portrait of Tsesarevich Alexei Petrovich* (1690–1718)

Anonymous artist. *Portrait of Tsesarevna Natalia Petrovna* (1718–1725)

Johann Gottrfried Tannauer. *Peter I on His Deathbed.* 1725

The New Hermitage

History and Architecture

The idea to build the New Hermitage, a museum accessible to the public, that would gather within its walls the artistic treasures of the Imperial family previously dispersed in the collections of the Tauride and Anichkov Palaces, summer residences at Tsarskoye Selo and Peterhof, the Small and Old Hermitage and other royal palaces, belonged to Nicholas I. It was his response to the novel cultural policy of Europe initiated after the fall of Napoleon and inspired by the democratization of society. The cultured public could now for the first time see what had been available only to the narrow circle of the "chosen" ones. It was on Nicholas's orders that in 1842–1851 the site near the Winter Palace was used for the construction of a new museum that completed the architectural complex of the St Petersburg Imperial residence. It occupied the area between the Small Hermitage and Winter Canal where all the dilapidated structures of Catherine's time had been demolished. Its northern facade adjoined the Old Hermitage while its main facade overlooked Millionaya Street.

The architect chosen to design the building was Leo von Klenze, responsible for the two famous Bavarian museums, the Pinakothek and the Glyptothek in Munich, built to accommodate paintings and sculptures of King Ludwig I. Nicholas I attended the Munich museums in 1838 and, greatly impressed by them, commissioned Leo von Klenze to design the "Imperial Museum" in St Petersburg.

Part of the New Hermitage portico

◄ **New Hermitage**

State Staircase

The task set by the Russian monarch surpassed in scale and complexity all the architect's previous projects. He was to embody in the New Hermitage, the first art museum in Russia, the most progressive ideas of a museum as a universal repository of the artistic experience of mankind. The huge Imperial collections were to be arranged in it according to a well-devised system allowing visitors to get the fullest possible notion of the history of world art. Moreover, Nicholas I made an express demand that the facades and interiors of the Imperial Museum should have a luxurious appearance befitting the status of an Imperial residence.

Klenze designed the New Imperial Hermitage as a museum within the museum. His building harmoniously blended various

Bertel (Albert) Thorvaldsen.
Shepherd. After 1817. Marble

State Staircase. Upper landing

The State Staircase

The wide and gently descending State Staircase divided into three flights builds up an impressive perspective in which the white marble steps and the beautiful yellow stuccowork (artificial marble) on the walls contrast effectively with the rose polished granite colonnades of the first-floor vestibule. The effect is heightened by streams of light on either side of the stairway. The twenty majestic elegant columns of Serdobol granite support the coffered ceiling and rhythmically complete the slender and chromatically exquisite architectural composition of the main staircase.

From 1861 onwards it was used for a large display of the collection of Western European sculpture of the late 18th and early 19th centuries. Many of these statues were acquired for Nicholas I. Most of them were commissioned to the sculptors of Rome and Florence on the order of the emperor. The most remarkable exhibits are works by the leading sculptors of Neoclassicism, Antonio Canova and Bertel Thorvaldsen. Well represented is the oeuvre of the generation that followed Canova, i.e. Pietro Tenerani, Lorenzo Bartolini, Giovanni Dupre, Luigi Bienaime and others.

forms and genres of the fine arts and architecture. The exterior of the majestic palace designed in a Neo-Greek style was adorned with an impressive architectural symbol — a portico with ten granite atlantes.

It is mainly to Leo von Klenze that we owe the imposing ensemble of the New Hermitage museum interiors and the fascinating sense of integrity characteristic of the building, despite all the wealth and variety of its decor (the unique decor of each room, gallery and study of the New Hermitage closely followed Klenze's plans).

According to the general plan, the magnificent rooms of the second floor of the New Hermitage were given for the richest, world-famous collections of Western Euro-

Giovanni Dupre (1817–1882). *Abel.* 1844. Marble

Room of Italian Majolica (Raphael Room)

Room of Italian Majolica (Raphael Room)

The Room of Italian Majolica (Raphael Room) and Cabinets

The design of the entire suite of rooms running parallel to the Raphael Loggias, from the present-day Room of Italian Majolica to the Knights Room and the Twelve-Column Hall, was even more decorative and varied. The polychrome painted decoration of the walls and ceilings, the reliefs and mouldings, as well as the unique inlaid parquet floors made up a fine setting for the collections they held. The Italian Majolica Room (on the second floor of the New Hermitage) houses not only unique specimens of this form of applied art but also works by the two geniuses of the Renaissance – Raphael and Michelangelo. This room blends together the ideal world of Renaissance art with the dramatic Baroque age. Small Cabinets, next to the Italian Skylight Halls, accommodate Italian painting and sculpture from the 17th and 18th centuries. This suite of rooms is completed by the Room of Raphael's Frescoes.

Room of Raphael's Frescoes

Knights Room

The Knights Room

In one of the spacious rooms adjoining the Skylight Halls, so-called Munzkabinett, the architect Leo von Klenze displayed an enormous Imperial numismatic collection.

The decor of the interior was unusual and highly expressive. The ceiling was abundantly painted with ornaments, the walls lined with panels made of artificial marble, the multi-coloured parquet floor was composed of a variety of costly types of wood.

Now this interior is known as Knights Room; it houses the celebrated Hermitage collection of Western European arms and armour dating from the 15th to 17th centuries.

pean paintings from the 17th and 18th centuries. The imposing State Staircase joins them to the collections of Antiquity that can be seen in the rooms of the first floor, specially designed for their display. Klenze was at his best in the decor of this part of the interiors.

Apart from Klenze, an important role in the creation of the New Hermitage was played by the Building Commission that included the leading architects and engineers of St Petersburg. Two of its members, the architects Vasily Stasov and Nikolai Yefimov, were in fact the designer's co-authors as they carried out his project and made some amendments to it.

The New Hermitage was ceremoniously opened on 5 February 1852. The first visitors saw the exhibitions of ancient and modern sculpture mounted on the first floor and then ascended the formal marble staircase to enter the picture gallery. The celebration started with a performance given at the Hermitage Theatre and was completed by a ceremonial

Hall of Dionysus

dinner in one of the lavish and spacious halls of the museum.

In the first years of the museum's existence, admittance to the New Hermitage was strictly regimented as the museum, in the words of Nicholas I, was "a part and continuation of the royal residence." However, soon it became easier to get to the museum, and during the reign of Alexander II the first Director of the Hermitage Stepan Gedeonov obtained permission to allow free entry to all those who desired to visit the museum.

Roman Courtyard. Exhibition of Roman Decorative Sculpture: 1st – 2nd Centuries

The Rooms of Ancient Art

Guided by the idea to create an ultimately harmonious environment for a display of ancient and contemporary marble sculpture, decorative vases, small-scale statuary, coins, medals and gems of the Ancient World, the architect subtly stylized the historical setting in which these works had been originally used. For instance, he placed the collections of Greek and Roman small-scale sculpture on the sides of the Main Foyer imitating the shapes of an ancient peristyle (courtyard), a typical feature of a rich Hellenistic and Roman house.

The Dionysus Hall, lined with red artificial marble, reproduces the appearance of an ancient gallery, the longitudinal walls of which are divided by powerful pillars, the floor is embellished with polychrome mosaics and the ceiling decor is stylized in the manner of ancient coffered interiors. This hall houses a display of ancient white marble statues.

The appearance of the next room, the Aura Hall, reproduces the peristyle courtyard. The eight snow-white fluted columns of Carrara marble are highlighted by the pale lilac stuccowork of the walls. Around them, similarly to the ancient times, are arranged museum statues, which were an indispensable part of interior decoration. The balance of proportions in the manner of Classical Antiquity is characteristic of the sculptures' pediments, showcases, sofas and armchairs intended for visitors and executed in the Neo-Greek style after designs by Leo von Klenze.

The similar effect of a synthesis of architectural interior and museum display is also present in the Twenty-Column and Jupiter Halls. The severe Classical stylization of the decor of the first-floor rooms in the New Hermitage somewhat sets off the noble beauty of antique statues, making this interior the highest achievement of 19th-century museum architecture.

The huge space of the Jupiter Hall recalls by its scale the living apartments of the Roman emperors. The huge flat vault decorated with polychrome reliefs rests on the mighty pylons projecting from the walls. They are trimmed with artificial marble of dark green tone in imitation of quadriums with free patterns of texture. The white marble statues of ancient gods, sarcophagi and busts of Roman emperors are set up against the background of the longitudinal wall in deep recessions formed by the pylons. The overall decorative effect is enhanced thanks to the inlaid parquet floor executed in the technique of Florentine mosaics.

Klenze skilfully stylized the Twenty-Column Hall as an ancient temple by dividing the space with two rows of monumental Ionic columns. The hall was designed for a display of the collection of Greek and Etruscan vases, so Klenze included in the decor of the walls, rafters and coffers ornamental, foliate and multi-figured motifs inspired by ancient vase painting. A real masterpiece and exhibit in its own right is the mosaic floor made in the very complex Venetian terrazzo technique by craftsmen of the Peterhof Lapidary Works.

In accordance with Klenze's original idea, the Room of the Large Vase was to serve as the main vestibule of the New Hermitage. Even before its walls were built, the largest in the world Kolyvan Vase (weight 19 tons) had been installed here. It had taken the Altai carvers fourteen years to make the vase. The vehicle that carried it was driven by 160 horses.

Hall of Jupiter

Room of Tauride Venus

Kolyvan Vase. 1843. Designed by Alexei Melnikov. Altai, Kolyvan Lapidary Works. Jasper; carving. Height 2.57 m

Gallery of the History of Ancient Painting

The Gallery of the History of Ancient Painting

According to Klenze's concept, the Gallery of the History of Ancient Painting was to anticipate visitors' meeting with authentic mas-

Antonio Canova. *Cupid and Psyche.* 1796. Marble

ANTONIO CANOVA
1757–1822

The second-floor rooms of the New Hermitage start with an excellent architectural piece – the Gallery of the History of Ancient Painting. It accommodates a comprehensive collection of European sculpture dating from the late 18th – early 19th centuries, the period of Neoclassicism. Antonio Canova is recognized as the founder of this style in sculpture. The Gallery of the History of Ancient Painting displays fifteen works by the great Italian master who had numerous followers in Europe. Even in his lifetime this artist became an idol of art patrons and collectors, among them French Emperor Napoleon Bonaparte, Russian Emperor Alexander I and many others. After the death of Napoleon's first wife Josephine de Beauharnais, in 1814, Alexander I purchased a fine collection of her Malmaison Palace near

Paris. Together with thirty-eight paintings by European artists it contained four first-rate marble statues created by Canova on Josephine's commission: *Cupid and Psyche*, *Dancer*, *Hebe* and *Paris*. They demonstrate a variety of subjects that attracted the sculptor and are highly characteristic of his manner. The *Three Graces*, a harmonious sculptural group and an implementation of perfect beauty, is probably the most popular piece by Canova. It was also commissioned for the Malmaison Palace but the commissioner did not live to see the masterpiece by her favourite artist. It was inherited by Josephine's son, Eugene de Beauharnais. In the early 20th century the sculptural group came to the Hermitage from the collection of Eugene's descendant, Duke of Leuchtenberg.

Antonio Canova. *The Three Graces.* 1813. Marble

terpieces of European art displayed in the New Hermitage, and the legendary history of art recorded on the walls was to introduce visitors into the world's artistic process and European cultural space. The dominant feature of the gallery decor is eighty-six unique paintings executed in the ancient medium of encaustic, or the application of colours with hot wax on copperplates. Produced by the Munich painter Georg Hiltensperger, they deal with events from ancient history and various legendary subjects. The pictures illustrate the origin of art in Antiquity, discoveries and achievements of ancient painters, invention of diverse techniques and technologies of painting, the flowering of art in Ancient Greece and its eventual decline in Ancient Rome during the period of the barbarians' invasions.

Antonio Canova. *Hebe.* 1800–05. Marble

Large Italian Skylight Hall

The Skylight Halls

The three Skylight Halls make up the main suite of striking magnificence located on the second floor of the New Hermitage. They owe their names to the unique type of giant vaulted ceilings crowned with glazed lanterns through which light floods into the halls. It was in the Skylight Halls that the largest paintings, for which daylight was thought to be most favourable, were hung. The walls painted in the intense dark red colour provide a fine setting for a majestic display of large-scale canvases of the Italian and Spanish schools, as they also did in the reign of Nicholas I. In the noble shining of gilded mouldings of the vaults masterpieces by the Great Masters perfectly blend with numerous luxurious tables, vases, lamp stands fashioned of semiprecious stones, settees upholstered in red velvet and armchairs of gilded wood.

Decor and Furnishing

The vast spaces of the walls in the Skylight Halls are painted in dark red; they were originally covered with the fabric of the same colour. The environment is much contributed to by the furniture designed in minute detail by Leo von Klenze in cooperation with other architects and all sorts of decorative objects made of Urals malachite, porphyry, rhodonite, jasper and lapis lazuli. They were produced on special commissions from the Hermitage by the then famous lapidary works of the Altai, Urals and Peterhof. The Altai stones, many of which were well known all over the world, were carved at the Kolyvan Lapidary Works.

The set of a vase and two lamp stands adorning the Small Spanish Skylight Hall of the New Hermitage is an outstanding specimen of decorative and applied art. The large porphyry bowl decorated with a splendid carved ornament is supported by three figures of winged chimeras made of porphyry and gilded bronze. Though all the pieces have many metal elements, stone is much more important for their decorative aspect. To the left and right of the vase are two lamp stands in the shape of columns fashioned to a design by the architect Andrei Voronikhin who played a significant part in the development of the lapidary's arts in Russia.

Small Spanish Skylight Hall.
Standard lamps and vase. 1805–07, 1811. Altai, Kolyvan Lapidary Works. Korgon porphyry and bronze; carving and gilding. Height of lamp stands 240 cm; height of vase 183 cm

Small Italian Skylight Hall

Raphael Loggias

The Raphael Loggias

On the side of the Winter Canal the Skylight Halls are adjoined by a long gallery which is a replica of the Raphael Loggias in the Vatican palace. Built in the 16th century by the celebrated architect Bramante and decorated with frescoes by Raphael and his pupils, it was reproduced in St Petersburg at the behest of Catherine the Great in 1783–1792. Giacomo Quarenghi made all necessary architectural measurements in Rome and put up the building in St Petersburg (next to the Old Hermitage and opposite the Hermitage Theatre) according to them.

Even before the beginning of the construction Catherine II ordered to make copies of Raphael's frescoes. They were commissioned from the Roman painter Christoph Unterberger, who faithfully transferred, together with his assistants, the great artist's Vatican masterpieces onto canvas. In 1787–88 the canvases were fixed in the interiors of the Raphael Loggias. Thus the Hermitage came to possess a unique version of the almost lost today famous Renaissance ensemble of frescoes.

Paintings

The gallery consists of thirteen sections or loggias. The light flooding through the arches (in the Vatican they are not glassed) is reflected in the mirrors of the opposite wall and creates an effect of endless light-filled space. The walls and vaults of the loggias are covered with fanciful grotesque ornaments created by Raphael under the influence of ancient paintings which he had studied during excavations of Ancient Rome. The strict symmetry of the arrangement of different elements does not make the paintings seem immobile, as no element is repeated twice. Harmoniously included into the overall composition of the loggias, the painted images are sometimes called "Raphael's Bible." Each vault has four paintings on biblical subjects – from the Creation of the world and the story of Adam and Eve to the Crucifixion of Christ.

The Vatican reliefs of the bottom part are replaced in the St Petersburg loggias with grisaille paintings.

Vault painting

Wall painting

This complex was born for the second time in the middle of the 19th century. During the construction of the New Hermitage some auxiliary structures and the building with the loggias were to be dismantled and the paintings executed in the 18th century on canvases removed. However, the idea of complete dismantlement of Quarenghi's complex was given up. Vasily Stasov and Nikolai Yefimov, who assisted him, introduced certain alterations into Klenze's plan, which allowed including most important of the extant structures into the complex of the New Hermitage. In Catherine's time Quarenghi's block had comprised a number of rooms but only the Raphael Loggias were recreated in the new Imperial Museum.

The foundation and walls of the previous structure were preserved; the paintings removed and later re-installed in the newly constructed gallery. The famous copies of the Vatican frescoes by the great Renaissance master became integral part of the Imperial Museum. The Raphael Loggias perfectly fitted into the architectural design of the New Hermitage and matched its interiors.

Wall painting

Italian Art: 16th – 18th Centuries

SECOND FLOOR: ROOMS 227, 229–238

The collection of Italian painting and sculpture from the 16th – 18th centuries is exhibited in the two main rooms of the New Hermitage, i.e. Large and Small Italian Skylight Halls, as well as in the next smaller cosy Cabinets and Room of Italian Majolica. The gems of the Hermitage collection are the *Crouching Boy*, a small sculpture by Michelangelo, and two paintings (the *Connestabile Madonna* and the *Holy Family*) by Raphael, the greatest Renaissance artist. The museum owns only one doubtless piece by the Late Renaissance painter, Tintoretto, that is the *Birth of St John the Baptist*, and one canvas by Michelangelo Merisi da Caravaggio, a great innovator of Italian art and at the same time follower of Renaissance traditions (*Lute Player*). A powerful artistic movement dominated the European art scene in the 17th century – it was the Baroque style. Many 16th-century Italian artists, first of all Caravaggio, contributed to its emergence. The great founder of the Baroque style in sculpture, Gian Lorenzo Bernini, is represented in the Hermitage by a series of terracotta studies for his well-known marble works.

In the 17th – 18th centuries Italy was gradually losing its leading position in European art and culture and sharing it with Spain, Flanders, Holland and France. The only exclusion was Venice. This majestic city was not much affected either by wars or economical troubles which had such an unfavourable impact on the rest of Italy. For a long time before it was invaded by Napoleon, this independent aristocratic republic had remained a luxurious shining world of infinite carnivals and sumptuous celebrations. This is how Venice is shown in *vedute*, detailed townscapes, the type of painting developed in the city.

The most celebrated Venetian master of painting in the 18th century was Giovanni Battista Tiepolo. The five large-scale paintings in the Hermitage collection based on subjects from ancient history were intended for the decoration of a hall in the palace of the Dolfino family in Venice. The gorgeous sunset of Italian painting, which received an outstanding embodiment in the work of Giovanni Battista Tiepolo, still continued to shed light upon all kinds of the fine arts in the course of the entire 18th century.

◀ **Large Italian Skylight Hall**

Dish. 16th century. Italy, Deruta. Majolica; painting over opaque white tin glaze, lustre. Diameter. Diameter 24 cm
"Wedding dish":
Camilla Bella.
1537. Italy, Casteldurante. Majolica; painting over opaque white tin glaze, lustre. Diameter 24 cm

The age of the Renaissance distinguished itself by the supreme level of workmanship in all kinds of art. The Hermitage owns about five hundred superb examples of majolica (painted and fired earthenware covered with coloured glazing) – dishes, vases and other vessels. Of particular interest are the so-called "wedding dishes" or "plates for lovers." In the centre of the bright-coloured dish, decorated with a polychrome ornament, was usually placed a half-length female representation skirted by a band with the name of the girl.

Michelangelo Bounarroti.
The Crouching Boy. Circa 1530. Marble. Height 54 cm

MICHELANGELO BUONARROTI
1475–1564

The genius of the Renaissance Michelangelo was an outstanding sculptor, architect, painter and poet. Almost all of his best works are to be found in Italy. The only example of his sculptural legacy in the Hermitage collection, the *Crouching Boy*, dates to the later period of his creative career and is probably connected with his work at the Medici Capella in Florence. This small marble piece clearly shows the master's typical creative device characteristic of his best sculptural works. The bent body of the boy is reminiscent of a tightly twisted spring charged with immense energy and at the same time his facial features, hands and feet are barely suggested as if tragically bound in torpid arrest. The boy's complex emotional state which combines suffering, concentration and introspection is conveyed through the rhythm of the sculptural masses and through the expressive play of light and shade on the hollows and swells of the marble block. Thus the work by this titan of the Renaissance reflects the forthcoming crisis of the harmonious, life-asserting ideal put forward during the Renaissance period.

Raphael (Rafaello Santi). *Conestabile Madonna.* Late 1502 – early 1503. Tempera on canvas (transferred from panel). 17.5 x 18 cm

RAPHAEL (RAFAELLO SANTI)
1483–1520

During his short lifetime Raphael succeeded in painting dozens of masterpieces – undoubted superb examples of High Renaissance art. The *Conestabile Madonna* (the picture's title comes from the name of its former owner) was evidently painted when the artist still lived in his native Perugia. The small-size painting has the shape of a tondo, i.e. the composition is placed into a circle. It also has a gorgeous frame made to a design of the artist.

Cassone. Mid-16th century. Venice. Wood; carving, painting and gilding

The frame used to be part of the original panel on which the picture was painted. In the 19th century the precious painting was transferred onto canvas.

In 1504 Raphael moved to Florence where he saw works by Leonardo da Vinci, which had a significant influence upon him. In his harmonious and calm *Holy Family* he created his ideal of feminine beauty based on his impressions of many beautiful faces he had ever seen in his life.

Raphael (Rafaello Santi). *The Holy Family (Madonna with Beardless Joseph).* Circa 1506. Tempera and oil on canvas. 72.5 x 56.5 cm

Widely represented in the Hermitage collection of Italian applied art are wooden bridal chests – *cassoni* in which the bride's dowry was kept. The shape of the chests goes back to ancient sarcophagi. Their side walls were usually embellished with skilfully painted or carved mythological subjects. The decor of this popular Renaissance type of the cabinet-maker's art was based on the elements borrowed from architecture.

Tintoretto (Jacopo Robusti). *The Birth of St John the Baptist.* Circa 1550. Oil on canvas. 181 x 266 cm

TINTORETTO (JACOPO ROBUSTI)
1518–1594

Tintoretto began his career in the workshop of Titian His painting combined Titian's exceptionally rich colour range and the power and expressiveness of Michelangelo's drawing. In his *Birth of St John the Baptist* the artist treats the Gospel subject as a mundane genre scene, in a full agreement with the Venetian Renaissance tradition.

ANNIBALE CARRACCI
1560–1609

The five paintings by Annibale Carracci on display in the Hermitage give us a notion of the artist's thematic range and his capacity as a painter. In the 1580s the Carracci (brothers Annibale and Agostino and their cousin Lodovico) opened in Bologna the *Accademia degli incaminati* ("the Academy of stepping on a right path"). This educational institution became the prototype of the future European art academies. The *Holy Women at the Sepulchre* is a fine example of large-scale multi-figured composition.

Annibale Carracci. *The Holy Women at the Sepulchre.* Second half of the 1590s. Oil on canvas. 121 x 145.5 cm

Caravaggio (Michelangelo Merisi da Caravaggio). *The Lute Player.*
Circa 1595. Oil on canvas. 94 x 119 cm

CARAVAGGIO (MICHELANGELO MERISI DA CARAVAGGIO)
1571–1610

The dynamism and emotional tension of the great master laid the basis for the stylistic principles of Baroque painting. It is primarily with Caravaggio that a special democratic tendency in European art, a distinct sort of realism that became widespread in the 17th century, is associated. He had most loyal followers in all European countries. Caravaggio's formative influence on his contemporaries could be compared only with the impact exercised on the art of their times by the titans of the Renaissance. One of Caravaggio's masterpieces is the famous *Lute Player*, in which, using the device of enhancing the contrasts of light and shade, the artist attains a great sense of volume, an almost illusory material, three-dimensional quality of the pictorial form.

Gian Lorenzo Bernini.
The Ecstasy of St Teresa.
1640s. Terracotta.
Height 47 cm

GIAN LORENZO BERNINI
1598–1680

The highest achievements of Baroque sculpture and architecture are associated with the name of Bernini. He became the leading sculptor and architect of Rome in his youth and decorated the Eternal City with a number of masterpieces. Bernini is represented in the Hermitage by a series of his *bozzetti* – terracotta studies for his well-known marble works.

Luca Giordano. *The Battle between the Lapiths and Centaurs.* Circa 1688. Oil on canvas. 255 x 390 cm

Giuseppe Mazzuolla. *The Death of Adonis.* 1709 Marble. Height 193 cm

LUCA GIORDANO
1632–1705

A marvellous example of decorative Baroque art, the *Battle between the Lapiths and Centaurs*, was based on Ovid's *Metamorphoses*. The Centaurs, invited to the wedding of the Lapiths' king, sought to steal the bride and her friends. Thus began a great battle, in which the Centaurs were defeated. The large canvas by Giordano is filled with battling figures. The centaur's broad croup depicted in the foreground seems to project from the picture, a characteristic feature of Baroque art, which tends to break down the borders between the illusory and real worlds.

GIUSEPPE MAZZUOLLA
1644–1725

Mazzuolla was Bernini's pupil. The *Death of Adonis* composition is a typical example of the decorative sculpture of the late Baroque period. The subject is taken from Ovid's *Metamorphoses*. It represents the tragic death of the beautiful youth Adonis, beloved of the goddess Venus, during a wild boar hunt.

Alessandro Magnasco (Lissandrino). *Banditti at Rest.* From the series done in 1710 (?). Oil on canvas. 112 x 162 cm

ALESSANDRO MAGNASCO (LISSANDRINO)
1667–1749

In the 17th century the realistic tendencies manifested in Caravaggio's painting received a specific transformation in intimate works of some talented artists active in Genoa, Bologna and Naples. The work of the Genoese artist Alessandro Magnasco is marked by a truly romantic predilection for subjects conveying the dark and excited state of his spirit.

ANTONIO CANAL (CANALETTO)
1697–1768

In the townscapes of Canaletto the "gem" of the Adriatic is represented in all the grandeur of its feast of life. The *Reception of the French Ambassador* is set in front of the Doges Palace. The sunlight plays on the rosy marble of its walls, emphasizing the bright colours of the clothes of the crowd on the Grand Canal embankment and of the visitors' costly attire.

Antonio Canal (Canaletto). *The Reception of the French Ambassador in Venice.* 1726. Oil on canvas. 181 x 259.5 cm

Giovanni Battista Tiepolo. *Maecenas Presenting the Liberal Arts to Emperor Augustus.* Circa 1745. Oil on canvas. 69.5 x 89 cm

GIOVANNI BATTISTA TIEPOLO
1696–1770

In comparison to the imposing Hermitage paintings created by Tiepolo for the palace of the Dolfino family in Venice his small-scale allegoric *Maecenas Presenting the Liberal Arts to Emperor Augustus* appears modest at first glance, but it is precisely this work that gives a full notion of his mastery as a painter. It belongs to Tiepolo's mature period and is remarkable for the unusual wealth and freshness of its colour range. The subject of the work is connected with the real figure – the Roman senator Gaius Cilnius Maecenas who gained such a fame for his patronage of artists that his name became a common noun. The picture was commissioned and dedicated to the celebration of Augustus III, Elector of Saxony.

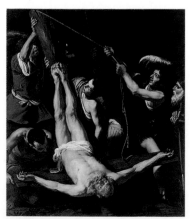

Lionello Spada (?). *The Martyrdom of St Peter.* First quarter of the 17th century. Oil on canvas. 232 x 201 cm

LIONELLO SPADA
1704–1739

The painting *Martyrdom of St Peter* ascribed to Spada would seem to be based on a lost work by Caravaggio. Subjects from the life of the patron of the Eternal City, the Apostle Peter, were very popular in Roman art. The Pope, head of the Catholic Church, is seen as St Peter's deputy on earth. According to legend, Peter was martyred on the Vatican Hill, crucified upside down by pagans.

Francesco Guardi. *View of the Island of San Giorgio Maggiore in Venice.* Between 1765 and 1775. Oil on canvas. 43 x 61 cm

FRANCESCO GUARDI
1712–1793

Guardi was a most refined Venetian artist, a great master of the townscape – known as *vedute* in Italian. In his works even modest corners of Venice look unforgettably beautiful. He painted many views of the island of San Giorgio Maggiore in Venice, where one of the richest monasteries was founded at the end of the 10th century. Guardi shows the island from the embankment by the Doges Palace, from where the facade of the church built by the leading 16th-century Italian architect Andrea Palladio is best seen.

BERNARDO BELOTTO
1722–1780

View of Pirna from the Right Bank of the Elbe belongs to a series of views of Dresden and the small neigbouring town of Pirna. It consists of fifteen paintings and is known as Bruhl's series as it was created by Belotto for Count Heinrich von Bruhl, minister to the court of the Elector of Saxony Augustus III. Bellotto's work reveals the best qualities of the Venetian painterly style in the conveyance of the almost transparent water and the buildings reflected in it, the softly melting background and the briefly sketched figures in the foreground.

Bernardo Belotto. *View of Pirna from the Right Bank of the Elbe.* Circa 1753. Oil on canvas. 133 x 237.5 cm

Spanish Art: 15th – 19th Centuries

SECOND FLOOR: ROOMS 239–240

The Small Spanish Skylight Hall and one of the Cabinets next to it display a not very large (150 paintings), yet comprehensive collection of Spanish art, mainly from the 17th century. While Italian art had always been popular in Europe, a real interest in Spanish painting aroused only in the 19th century, after the Napoleonic Wars, when paintings by major artists, previously kept in the monasteries, cathedrals and palaces began to be taken abroad from the devastated Spain and put on sale in Paris and London. Most of the Spanish works entered the Hermitage holdings in 1814 from Baron Coesvelt's collection (Amsterdam).

The 17th century is usually regarded as the heyday of Spanish painting. Its beginning was marked by the great El Greco (Domenikos Theotokopoulos). The Hermitage owns two works by the artist, one of them being the world-famous *Apostles Peter and Paul.*

The greatest achievements of 17th-century Spanish art include paintings by Diego Velazquez, Jose de Ribera, Francisco de Zurbaran and Bartolome Esteban Murillo. Six paintings by Jose de Ribera open up the era of the "golden age" in the Hermitage collection of Spanish art. The Hermitage has two works (*Luncheon* and *Portrait of Olivares*) by the most celebrated Spanish artist Velazquez and four pieces by Zurbaran. His *Childhood of the Virgin* is one of a few lyrical paintings in the oeuvre of this usually austere master restrained in his emotions. The Hermitage owns a most representative collection (about twenty works) by Murillo reflecting all the phases of his work. The museum also boasts *Portrait of the Actress Antonia Sarate* created by the greatest master Francisco Goya who lived at the turn of the 18th and 19th centuries and started the new epoch of revolutionary transformations in European painting.

◀ **Small Spanish Skylight Hall**

Anonymous Spanish artist of the Castilian school. Second half of the 15th century.
The Entombment. Tempera and oil on panel. 94 x 182 cm

ANONYMOUS SPANISH ARTIST OF THE CASTILIAN SCHOOL

The painting was once kept in a small village church in the environs of Valladolid. Originally it was part of *retablos* – a large-scale decorative altar structure including paintings, pieces of sculpture and architectural details. The central part of the panel on which the picture was painted has not survived. Probably it supported some architectural detail or sculpture of the *retablos*. Domi-

nant in the horizontal composition is the body of Christ carefully supported by the Virgin, St Nicodemus, St Mary Magdalene, St John the Evangelist and St Joseph of Arimathea. In front of the sarcophagus are depicted plants bearing symbolic message: irises as a symbol of sorrow, carnations as a sign of shed blood, lilies as an allegory of purity and roses with thorns as an allusion to the Passion. The customer who commissioned the painting is shown below right; his coat-of-arms can be seen on the left side of the sarcophagus.

ANONYMOUS ARTIST

Spanish religious painting strictly followed the church canon rules. Two early Christian martyrs who lived in the 3rd century are shown with their traditional attributes: St Fabian with a sword and St Sebastian with arrows. Fabian, the Pope of Rome, was one of the first to be martyred for Christ in the cause of cruel persecutions of the adherents of the new religion. Legend holds that St Sebastian, a former centurion, helped his brothers and sisters in Christ and was killed with arrows also during a persecution of Christians.

Anonymous artist. *Sts Fabian and Sebastian.* Between 1475 and 1500. Oil and tempera on panel. 141.4 x 89.5 cm

LUIS DE MORALES
Between 1520 and 1525–1585

The artist may have spent all his life in the Spanish region of Extremadura where he worked on commissions of local churches and monasteries. The agitation and tragic exaltation characteristic of Morales' religious works were the result of a certain mystical teaching widespread in Spain in the 16th century. That teaching renounced the role of Church as mediator between Christians and the Lord.

His *Virgin and Child with a Cross-Shaped Distaff* was probably created under the influence of Leonardo da Vinci's paintings – engravings made after them were popular in Spain at the period.

Luis de Morales. *The Virgin and Child with a Cross-Shaped Distaff.* Oil on canvas. 71.5 x 52 cm

JUAN PANTOJA DE LA CRUZ
1533–1608

Juan Pantoja de la Cruz was court painter to Kings Philip II and Philip III. He painted many portraits of representatives of the haughty and arrogant Spanish aristocracy – the rigid flat figures, clad in luxurious garments with orders and gems against a dark background.

The *Portrait of Diego de Villamayor* is one of the best works in his legacy. The sitter was a scion of the aristocratic family whose origins went as far back as the 11th century. The Order of the Alcantara which could be worn only by the chosen few suggests the noble origin of the seventeen-year-old grandee.

Juan Pantoja de la Cruz. *Portrait of Diego de Villamayor.* 1605. Oil on canvas. 89 x 71 cm

El Greco (Domenikos Theotokopoulos). *The Apostles Peter and Paul.* Between 1587 and 1592. Oil on canvas. 121.5 x 105 cm

EL GRECO (DOMENIKOS THEOTOKOPOULOS)
1541–1614

A Greek by origin, the artist came to Venice in his early years and began to work at the studio of Titian, studying also the art of Tintoretto and Veronese. In search of commissions he went to Rome. In the 1570s he moved to Spain and started working in Toledo that was in opposition to the royal court.

The world-famous *Apostles Peter and Paul* is the first work in the *Apostolados* series dedicated to Christ and the twelve apostles. He painted it when already at Toledo. The hands of Sts Peter and Paul form a perfectly found compositional and ideological centre of the painting.

ALONSO SANCHEZ COELLO
1531/32–1588

Coello was court painter to King Philip II. He did likenesses of the king, members of his family and representatives of the aristocracy. The artist introduced a certain canon for the national type of court portrait. The sitter should be static and the background neutral. All the details of the costume must be meticulously rendered and the model should not be idealized. The Hermitage works by Alonso Sanchez Coello and his pupil Juan Pantoja de la Cruz enable us to appreciate the refined aristocratic elegance and noble restraint characteristic of the best examples of Spanish portraiture.

Alonso Sanchez Coello. *Portrait of the Infanta Catalina Michaela of Austria.* Between 1582 and 1585. Oil on canvas. 70 x 50 cm

DIEGO VELAZQUEZ
1599–1660

Velazquez was the most celebrated Spanish artist and court painter to King Philip IV. He stood out among other artists thanks to his powerful, early matured talent, recognized and highly valued by his contemporaries. *Luncheon*, an early work of eighteen-year-old painter, belongs to the *bodegon* ("tavern") genre which was very popular in Spain. It betrays Caravaggio's influence. Velazquez depicts a usual tavern scene with real-life Spanish people having a modest meal. The scene is illuminated by a narrow stream of direct light in the manner of Caravaggio, which singles the group out against the semi-dark interior. However, Velazquez invests this seemingly everyday scene, in the same way as Caravaggio before him, with some additional meaning. The still-life objects in the foreground – a pomegranate, a loaf and a glass of wine – are Christian symbols, and the images of the boy, youth and old man can be associated with the three

Diego Velazquez. *Portrait of Count-Duke Olivares.* Circa 1640. Oil on canvas. 67 x 54.5 cm

periods in human life.

The likeness of Count-Duke Olivares ranks with undoubted masterpieces of Velazquez's portraiture. Don Gaspar de Guzman, Count Olivares, Duke of Sanlucar, was the mighty Prime-Minister of the royal court who patronized the young painter.

Diego Velazquez. *Luncheon.* Circa 1617–18. Oil on canvas. 108.5 x 102 cm

Francisco de Zurbaran. *St Lawrence.* 1636. Oil on canvas. 292 x 225 cm

FRANCISCO DE ZURBARAN
1598–1664

The entire career of this unique artist of most powerful talent is associated with his native Seville. His paintings used to decorate the cathedrals and monasteries of the city. Only a small number of works by this Spanish artist can be found outside Spain. Noteworthy among the Hermitage paintings by Zurbaran is *St Lawrence*, a rare monumental altarpiece. Legend has it that St Lawrence was the first deacon of the Roman Christian Church. The enemies of Christianity burnt him on an iron gridiron which became a symbol of the saint and can be seen in his numerous depictions. Zurbaran, following the Spanish tradition, does not idealize the saint but endows the image with distinctive national features.

In the *Childhood of the Virgin*, like in his other works treating religious themes, Zurbaran succeeds in naturally combining the protagonist's restraint and complete aloofness from all earthly things with few, but very expressive, distinctly Spanish details of life.

Francisco de Zurbaran. *The Childhood of the Virgin.* Circa 1658–1660. Oil on canvas. 73.5 x 53.5 cm

Jose de Ribera. *St Sebastian Cured by St Irene.* 1628. Oil on canvas. 156 x 188 cm

JOSE DE RIBERA
1591–1652

Ribera spent most of his lifetime in Naples which was then part of the Spanish Kingdom. He adopted all the best traditions of the Italian school of painting. His artistic manner is highly temperamental. The artist boldly and freely models his forms by energetic brushstrokes of restrained tones. The influence of his favourite master Caravaggio is manifested in the actively used *tenebroso* technique (dramatic emphasis on contrasting light-and-shade effects). The Hermitage paintings by Ribera showing saints of the Christian Church are recognized masterpieces.

Jose de Ribera. *St Onuphrius.* 1637. Oil on canvas.
130 x 104 cm

Bartolome Esteban Murillo. *Boy with a Dog.*
1650s. Oil on canvas. 74 x 60 cm

BARTOLOME ESTEBAN MURILLO
1617–1682

Paintings by the last master of the "golden age," Bartolome Esteban Murillo, were extremely popular with collectors of Spanish art. The Hermitage owns an extensive collection of his works representing all the three main periods in Murillo's oeuvre – "cold," "warm" and "airy." The *Boy with a Dog* dates from the early period when the artist eagerly painted gypsies, beggars, poor people who were in need yet optimistic and ingenious in revealing their feelings. The *Immaculate Conception*, a virtuoso painting in a light silver-blue gamut, executed boldly and freely, is a perfect example of the artist's "airy" manner.

Bartolome Esteban Murillo. *The Immaculate Conception.* 1660s.
Oil on canvas. 236 x 197 cm

Antonio de Pereda. *Still Life.* 1652. Oil on canvas. 80 x 94 cm

ANTONIO DE PEREDA
1608–1678

The 17th century witnessed the flourishing of Spanish still life. Spanish artists endowed objects with a special elevated, spiritual atmosphere, thus suggesting an invisible presence of man in the kingdom of *nature morte*. One of the best Madrid painters of the middle of the 17th century, Antonio de Pereda seems to caress each object in his still life delighting in the transparency of the glass, the thickness and brightness of painted ceramic ware and the sheen of a metal vessel for boiling coffee. He skilfully juxtaposes their textures with the biscuits and cheese lying in the foreground.

FRANCISCO DE GOYA
1746–1828

One of the two portraits of the actress Antonia Sarate commissioned to Goya by her close friend Garcia de la Prada was presented to the Hermitage in 1973 by the American art collector Armand Hammer. Antonia was born to the family of an actor (Valdes Sarate) and started her career in the late 18th century. She was probably better known for her striking beauty than talent. Created by the great master, the emotional, touching image of the young woman, who would die at the age of thirty-six, is a sort of link between the lofty spiritual worlds of the "golden age" of Spanish art and the forthcoming age of Romanticism.

Francisco de Goya. *Portrait of Antonia Sarate.* Circa 1811. Oil on canvas. 71 x 58 cm

Flemish Art: 17th – 18th Centuries

SECOND FLOOR: ROOMS 245–248

Flanders as an independent state emerged on the map of Europe in the early 17th century. After a prolonged war for liberation that the Netherlands fought against Spain, which had been ruling the Low Countries, seven northern provinces gained independence and proclaimed the Dutch Republic. In the Southern Netherlands, then known as Flanders, after the name of the largest province, the rule of the Spanish governor-general survived. Netherlandish art fell apart into two independent national schools – Dutch and Flemish – which became leading centres of European culture.

The art of Flanders is exhaustively represented in the Hermitage. Its collection includes over 500 works in a variety of genres demonstrating the versatile mastery of 140 Flemish artists. The Hermitage boasts large collections by the leader of the Flemish school Peter Paul Rubens, famous portrait painter Anthony van Dyck, celebrated master of still lifes Frans Snyders, painter of large-scale decorative compositions Jacob Jordaens and artist of genre scenes David Teniers.

The flowering of Flemish painting in the first half of the 17th century is associated primarily with Peter Paul Rubens. His works in the Hermitage are represented in all variety of forms – altarpieces, sketches for large-scale decorative panels, portraits and landscapes. Anthony van Dyck enjoyed world-wide renown of the best portrait painter of Europe in his early years. He evolved a special type of formal portraits of monarchs and aristocracy. Unsurpassed in his painting skills, he was also a genius of psychological portrait. The uniqueness of Flemish art is manifested in the works by Jacob Jordaens, particularly in his most famous piece, the *Bean King*. Frans Snyders was long associated with Rubens and his studio. He became particularly famous as the painter of the *Stalls* series now in the Hermitage. Not a single European school of the 17th century has created anything on a par with these large-scale vigorous still lifes which seem to amass all the wealth of nature's riches – Snyders was justly called the "Rubens of still life."

Exhibition of Flemish Art.
Van Dyck Room

Peter Paul Rubens. *The Feast in the House of Simon the Pharisee.* Between 1618 and 1620. Oil on canvas. 189 x 284.5 cm

Peter Paul Rubens. *Perseus and Andromeda.* Early 1620s. Oil on canvas (transferred from panel). 99.5 x 139 cm

PETER PAUL RUBENS
1577–1640

Perseus and Andromeda, a masterpiece of the Hermitage collection, was painted by Peter Paul Rubens in one of the happiest periods in his life, when his art attained an unrivalled excellence. This painting is based on a mythological subject borrowed from Ovid's *Metamorphoses*. The Ancient Greek hero Perseus, son of Zeus and Danae, saves the daughter of the Ethiopian king, bound to a rock as a sacrifice to the sea monster. His *Feast in the House of Simon the Pharisee* depicts a repentant woman washing Christ's feet with costly aromatic oil and wiping them with her hair. Rubens's superb mastery permeates

Peter Paul Rubens. *The Union of Earth and Water.* Circa 1618. Oil on canvas. 222.5 x 180.5 cm

with living energy the most conventional allegoric compositions. In the *Union of Earth and Water* glorifying the union of the two elements Rubens expressed in an allegorical form a hope that "the lands of Flanders will again flourish" as soon as they had an access to the sea. His *Portrait of a Lady-in-Waiting* allows one to see a different, more profound and psychological, facet of Rubens's talent. This highly spiritual likeness has a resemblance to Clara Serena, Rubens's favourite daughter who died at the age of twelve. *Bacchus* ranks with the best works of Rubens's later period. The artist shows the ancient god of wine not in his usual image of a beautiful young man but as a fat reveller seated on a barrel.

Peter Paul Rubens. *Portrait of a Lady-in-Waiting to the Infanta Isabella.* Mid-1620s. Oil on panel. 64 x 48 cm

Peter Paul Rubens. *Bacchus.* Between 1638 and 1640. Oil on canvas (transferred from panel). 191 x 161.3 cm

Anthony van Dyck. *Self-Portrait.* Late 1620s – early 1630s. Oil on canvas. 166.5 x 93.5 cm

ANTHONY VAN DYCK
1599–1641

Van Dyck revealed his brilliant gift as a child – the son of a wealthy Antwerp burgher. In his young years he earned fame as the best portraitist of Europe.

The Hermitage paintings that demonstrate diverse facets of his talent date from different periods of his career. His *Family Portrait* was painted before his departure for Italy. His *Self-Portrait* was done on his return to Antwerp when Van Dyck was showered with a stream of commissions. Besides portraits, the artist was sometimes commissioned to paint religious subjects. A fine example is the Hermitage's painting *Madonna with Partridges or Rest on the Flight into Egypt* – one of few works of this kind in Van Dyck's legacy. This painting was probably commissioned by the "association of bachelors," a religious brotherhood dedicated to the Virgin Mary (Van Dyck was its member). The last, short London period is especially well represented in the Hermitage collection. The famous Flemish portrait painter stood at the beginning of the national English school of portraiture that would reach its heyday in the 18th century.

Anthony van Dyck. *Family Portrait.* Late 1621. Oil on canvas. 113.5 x 93.5 cm

Anthony van Dyck. *Rest on the Flight into Egypt (Madonna with Partridges).* Early 1630s.
Oil on canvas. 215 x 285.5 cm

Anthony van Dyck. *Portrait of Elizabeth and Philadelphia Wharton* (?).
Second half of the 1630s. Oil on canvas. 162 x 130 cm

Jacob Jordaens. *The Bean King.* Circa 1638. Oil on canvas. 157 x 211 cm

JACOB JORDAENS
1593–1678

Jacob Jordaens, a pupil of Peter Paul Rubens, became the recognized leader of the Flemish school after his teacher's death. His *Bean King* features the culmination of a popular folk festival of the Three Magi, or Three Kings, which was celebrated in Flanders every year on 6th January (Epiphany). During this day a large pie was baked in every home, with a bean put inside. The one who would find the bean in his piece of pie, was honoured as the "king" of the holiday. The spirit of Flanders and its people is embodied in the works of this very Flemish of all the artists.

FRANS SNYDERS
1579–1657

The famous "stalls" by Snyders were painted for the decoration of a dining room in the house of a Brussels official. Their compositions are typical of Snyders's manner. Nature's riches are crowded in the foreground of his large-scale canvases giving an impression that the latter can't accommodate them all. Striking for the richness of their colours and forms, they cover the tables, overfill the baskets, dishes and bowls and seem to be on the verge of falling to the feet of the viewer.

Frans Snyders. *Fish Market.* 1620s. Oil on canvas. 207 x 341 cm

Frans Snyders. *Greengrocery Stall.* Between 1618 and 1621. Oil on canvas.
208 x 341 cm

Frans Snyders. *Fruit Bowl.* 1650s.
Oil on panel. 71.6 x 103 cm

DAVID TENIERS II
1610–1690

The State Hermitage boasts one of the world's finest collections of works by the famous Flemish painter David Teniers II, the last great representative of this school. Over forty paintings from the time when the artist was at his peak demonstrate the main facets of his oeuvre and reveal the distinctive nature of his style. The country festival, a most popular subject of Flemish painting, is interpreted in Teniers's composition as some theatrical action.

David Teniers II. *Peasant Wedding.* 1650. Oil on canvas. 82 x 108 cm

Dutch Art: 17th – 18th Centuries

SECOND FLOOR: ROOMS 249–254

The Dutch school of painting was formed later than the Flemish one – by the 1630s, and the period of its highest development fell on the middle of the 17th century. Paintings by Dutch artists were always very popular with collectors and by the early 20th century the Hermitage possessed one of the largest collections of Dutch art. Long before the foundation of the museum, in 1716, Peter the Great acquired in Holland about two hundred works which were used to adorn his residence in the capital and suburban palaces. Peter's collection included one of Rembrandt's masterpieces, *David and Jonathan*, the first work by the great master to come to Russia. Today the Hermitage collection of Rembrandt's works may be called unique, without any exaggeration.

Most of the Dutch artists worked on commissions from local burghers who preferred to decorate the rooms of their homes, not large in size, with scenes of everyday life, portraits, still lifes and landscapes – all of small size. For this the artists were dubbed "Small Dutch Masters." They lived in Amsterdam, Haarlem, Utrecht, Delft, Leyden and The Hague and created "art of reality" which was widespread in Holland and had a distinct national flavour. Each artist specialized in some definite theme and there was a great variety of these themes. Painted with meticulous attention to detail, their pictures attracted the customers by their poetical, though devoid of idealization, interpretation of the everyday life of common townsfolk. They were distinguished by a subtle colour scheme, virtuoso rendering of light and air and textural variety of objects, in which 17th-century Dutch painters were unrivalled.

In his still lifes Pieter Claesz reveals great beauty and harmony of objects that surround people in their daily life. In his *Glass of Lemonade* Gerard Terborch has turned a scene with a procuress into a subtle and elevated world dominated by exquisite tones. Jan Steen illustrates a wide range of morals and customs characteristic of his contemporaries. The culmination of the development of Dutch art is the oeuvre of the excellent portrait painter Frans Hals.

◀ **Exhibition of Dutch Art.**
Tent-Roofed Room

Rembrandt Harmenszoon van Rijn. *Flora.* 1634. Oil on canvas. 125 x 101 cm

Rembrandt Harmenszoon van Rijn.
The Sacrifice of Isaac. 1635. Oil on canvas.
193 x 132 cm

REMBRANDT HARMENSZOON VAN RIJN
1606–1669

More than twenty priceless paintings owned by the Hermitage cover various phases in the master's complicated career throughout forty years – from his early works still painted in a traditional meticulous manner and winning success with the public to the philosophically profound and tragic later images which were understood only by rare like-minded people. These masterpieces demonstrate those peculiar features of his pictorial idiom which markedly differentiated Rembrandt

Rembrandt Harmenszoon van Rijn. *Danae.* 1636. Oil on canvas. 185 x 202.5 cm

from his Dutch contemporaries during his mature period. Created in different years, Rembrandt's paintings *Flora*, *David and Jonathan*, *Danae*, the *Sacrifice of Isaac*, the *Holy Family* and *David and Uriah* are his most important works eloquently expressing his creative credo. Turning to distant biblical and Gospel scenes and ancient myths, Rembrandt invested them with a profound dramatic feeling converting his characters into real, loving and suffering people.

Flora is a lyrical portrait of Rembrandt's wife Saskia shown as goddess of flowers and gardens. The artist evidently admires his young partner depicting her in a beautiful festive-looking dress, wearing a floral wreath. It was the happiest period in his life. Rembrandt was loved. He enjoyed popularity and was rich. Soon Saskia died and Rembrandt lost not only her but also his wealth and glory. *Danae*, completed after Sas-

kia's death, unveils reasons for the conflict between the artist and society. His works became too complicated, involved too deep psychological characteristics to be valued by his contemporaries as high as they deserved it.

Rembrandt Harmenszoon van Rijn.
The Holy Family. 1645. Oil on canvas.
117 x 91 cm

Rembrandt Harmenszoon van Rijn. *Portrait of an Old Man in Red.* Circa 1652–54. 108 x 86 cm

Rembrandt Harmenszoon van Rijn. *David and Jonathan.* 1642. Oil on panel. 73 x 61.5 cm

Rembrandt Harmenszoon van Rijn. *The Return of the Prodigal Son.* Circa 1668–69. Oil on canvas. 262 x 205 cm

The *Return of the Prodigal Son* is the summing up of the life of Rembrandt who was now alone and had lost his welfare and happiness. He had lost all, except his ability to create. Deep thoughts and suffering that had permeated the entire oeuvre of the artist, reached their acme in this canvas, as large as an altarpiece and devoid of any superficial details. Love, mercy, understanding and forgiveness are main spiritual values granted to man. This eternal truth which the artist has found in the result of his own great sufferings is convincingly expressed in his last and greatest painting.

Rembrandt Harmenszoon van Rijn. *David and Uriah* (?). Circa 1665. Oil on canvas. 127 x 116 cm

Frans Hals. *Portrait of a Young Man with a Glove.* Circa 1650. Oil on canvas. 80 x 66.5 cm

FRANS HALS
Between 1581 and 1585–1666

The great portrait painter of the 17th century Frans Hals is represented in the Hermitage by two outstanding examples of his work. Hals not only records the appearance of his model and his calm dignity characteristic of a burgher (which was appreciated by his contemporaries) in sweeping, virtuoso brushstrokes, without indulging in elaboration of detail, but also captures the instantly changing features of the character portrayed, his state of mind. The artist demonstrates in his portrait the pose, gesture, turn of the head and look characteristic of this person alone in a definite situation. At the same time all the characters depicted by Hals have something in common – they share energetic, frank attitude to life. This is what his *Young Man with a Glove* looks like.

AERT VAN DER NEER
1603/04–1677

The artist's genuine gift is best manifested in his landscapes with moonlight. His interest in light effects is, however, also demonstrated in the representations of sunrise and in a large group of paintings featuring the dramatic subject of night fires which gave rise to a new type of painting in Dutch art. Van der Neer's few lyrical winter landscapes are shown in twilight.

One of them is the *River in Winter*. His works did not enjoy great success in his lifetime, yet the artist had many followers after his death. In the 19th century his oeuvre was highly valued by German Romantic painters.

Aert van der Neer. *River in Winter.* Circa 1645. Oil on panel. 35.5 x 62 cm

Jan Jozefsz van Goyen. *Winter Scene near The Hague.* 1645. Oil on panel. 52 x 70 cm

JAN JOZEFSZ VAN GOYEN
1596–1656

Best features of Dutch landscapes from the first half of the 17th century are to be seen in the works of Jan Jozefsz van Goyen (there are twelve of his paintings in the Hermitage). In the *Winter Scene near The Hague* the pearly colour scheme allows conveying the impression of a single light-and-air milieu and the extremely low horizon makes the space of the picture much deeper, receding into the distance.

JACOB ISAAKSZ VAN RUISDAEL
1628/29–1682

The highest accomplishments of Dutch landscape painting are associated with Jacob van Ruisdael whose works show a profound philosophic interpretation of nature. In 17th-century Dutch painting, abundant in talented masters, the work of Jacob van Ruisdael can be compared in terms of its scale only with the art of his great contemporary Rembrandt. The Hermitage has eleven pictures by the outstanding artist, including his famous *Marsh*, a world masterpiece.

Jacob Isaksz van Ruisdael. *Marsh.* 1660s. Oil on canvas. 72.5 x 99 cm

JAN STEEN
1625/26–1679

Jan Steen used to record scenes from the life of common Dutchmen usually invested with some moral ideas, not indulging, though, in moralizing. They were easily understood by his contemporaries who could discern symbolic allusions. The painting *Revellers* is one of Steen's masterpieces. The subject looks like a well-performed mise-en-scene where the characters (the artist himself and his wife Margaret, daughter of the landscape painter Jan van Goyen) are absolutely convincing. The amusing situation, however, conceals a moral maxim about pernicious consequences of the improper mode of life.

Jan Steen. *Revellers.* Circa 1660. Oil on panel. 39 x 30 cm

Gerard Terborch. *A Glass of Lemonade.* 1660s. Oil on canvas (transferred from panel). 67 x 54 cm

GERARD TERBORCH
1617–1681

The best among six excellent works representing this superb colourist and a keen observer of the life of his contemporaries in the Hermitage collection is surely *A Glass of Lemonade*. The artist has turned a scene with a procuress introducing a girl to a young soldier into a subtle and elevated world dominated by exquisite combinations of colours.

GABRIEL METSU
1629–1667

Gabriel Metsu, influenced by both Steen and Terborch, combined in his work a democratic and vivid approach of the former with an elegance of the latter. The theme of the painting *Doctor's Visit* was one of the most popular subjects that illustrated the proverb: "Medicine is helpless where love is involved" and occurred in many works by Dutch genre painters.

Gabriel Metsu. *Doctor's Visit.* 1660s. Oil on canvas. 61.5 x 47.5 cm

PIETER DE HOOCH
1629 – after 1684

Pieter de Hooch succeeded in penetrating to the very essence of the Dutch burgher's personality lovingly emphasizing such features as harmony, calm and purity. The main character of his paintings is light pervading accurate Dutch interiors, courtyards and streets and revealing the beauty of the most common details – dresses, tableware, brickwork, foliage or the smooth water of a canal which also have a symbolical context. The work of Pieter de Hooch exerted a great influence on many Dutch artists who worked in Delft and Amsterdam.

Pieter de Hooch. *Mistress and Her Maid.* Circa 1660. Oil on canvas. 53 x 42 cm

Willem Claesz Heda. *Breakfast with a Crab.* 1648. Oil on canvas. 118 x 118 cm

WILLEM CLAESZ HEDA
1594 – between 1680 and 1682

The mastery of leading still life painters is fully revealed in the so-called "breakfast" scenes. This type developed from early Netherlandish group portraits of corporate members in which the forefront usually showed laid tables with an abundance of diverse hors-d'oeuvres. By no chance Dutch still-life paintings suggest a presence of man who seems to have just left the room a minute before.

WILLEM KALF
1619–1693

The work of Willem Kalf testifies to the change of taste that took place in Dutch society in the second half of the 17th century. The burghers who had become rich were now trying to decorate their homes with objects of applied art and paintings attesting to their wealth. *Dessert*, Kalf's true masterpiece, is usually put into the category of "luxurious still life." The traditional Dutch "breakfast" scene is filled here with valuable exotic objects.

Willem Kalf. *Dessert.* Oil on canvas. 105 x 87.5 cm

Western European Arms and Armour: 15th – 18th Centuries

The celebrated Hermitage collection of Western European Arms and Armour dating from the 15th – 17th centuries is displayed in the Knights Room of the New Hermitage. Started at the royal residence of Tsarskoye Selo in 1810 due to Alexander I's passion for the history of chivalry, this large and representative collection took shape in the first quarter of the 19th century. Enriched with acquisitions made in Europe in the 19th century, it was transferred in 1885 to the Hermitage. It comprises unique items demonstrating virtuoso techniques of decoration that were employed by the craftsmen of Italy, Germany, Spain and France. The collection's full armour, shields, hauberk half-armour, cold steel and firearms trace the main periods of the development of weaponry in Europe. In the late 14th – early 15th centuries the Gothic style was dominant in many European countries, which led to the introduction of so-called "Gothic" type of armour that had elongated forms and sharp ribs. Together with other items the armour was extremely heavy and weighted from 40 to 80 kg. The knights must have been very strong to wear such armour and needed special training which could prepare them for battles; so tournaments were organized in the times of peace. At first ordinary arms were used in them and many a knight were seriously wounded or even killed in the course of those competitions. Later a less harmful type of arms was invented and used for the tournaments. The battle armour was simple in design while the tournament armour was abundant in decoration – engraved, inlaid with precious metals and stones, chased and gilded. The Knights Room houses a "Cavalcade of Knights" display (with stuffed horses) that demonstrates different types of full armour.

◀ **Knights Room. Part of the "Cavalcade of Knights" display**

Morion helmet. Between 1605 and 1610. Germany. Steel; forging, engraving and gilding. Height 34 cm

Helmet. Between 1570 and 1590. Germany. Steel; forging, engraving and gilding. Height 37 cm

Burgonet open helmet. Pageant (rondache) shield and gauntlet. Circa 1560. Italy, Venice. Steel; forging, engraving and damascening with gold

Cuirass breastplate. 1580–85. Antonio Piccinino's workshop. Italy, Milan. Steel; chasing and gilding. Length 31 cm

Pageant (rondache) shield. 1570s. Italy, Milan. Diameter 58 cm

The late 15th century is known as the "golden age" of armour. The suit of armour became lighter, more comfortable and safer and was even more intricately decorated. For gilding the mixture of gold and quicksilver (mercury amalgam) was applied on the surface of the metal to be later heated in a furnace. The mercury evaporated and the gold strongly attached to the surface. For blueing the surface was treated with oil or acid, then heated. As a result it was covered with transparent film of different colours. The craftsmen also employed chasing and engraving.

The armourers designed an enclosed three-piece helmet. It consisted of a cylindrical skullcap, movable visor and gorget that ran into the flexible metal covering for the neck and shoulders of the knight. This was attached to the cuirass protecting the breast, while the arms were covered with paulettes, brassards, cubitieres and gauntlets. The "Maximilian" armour

there appeared helmets of the Burgundian type, or burgonets (probably first produced by craftsmen of Burgundy). They were used both by cavalry and foot soldiers. Though the latter preferred helmets of morion type (from the Spanish "morro" – skull). They had a crest or comb at the top and a flat brim, with edges slightly turned up. Such helmets are still worn by the Swiss Guards of the Pope.

Part of the "Cavalcade of Knights" display

invented by German craftsmen was considered the best. It was named after Emperor Maximilian I who supported his armour craftsmen. In the second half of the 16th century there was introduced half-armour which weighted less and provided greater mobility and better protection from firearms. At that time

Covering for the neck and shoulders. Early 17th century. Steel; forging, chasing and silver inlay. Height 24.5 cm

Pageant (rondache) shield. Between 1560 and 1570. Steel; chasing and gilding. Diameter 60 cm

Full armour. Mid-16th century. Workshop of Siebenburger and F. Schmidt. Germany, Nuremberg. Steel; forging, chasing and gilding

Dagger and sheath.
1570–1580. Italy, Venice or Rome. Steel, agate and silver; blueing, gold inlay and gilding. Length 46 cm

Rapier.
Circa 1600–05. Frederic Piccinino's workshop. Italy, Milan. Steel; chasing and engraving

The Knights Room showcases fine specimens of Western European side-arms: swords, daggers, sabers etc. Its numerous exhibits – from terrifying heavy mediaeval two-handle swords to refined, yet lethal sabres set with precious stones and inlaid with gold, elegant stilettos and daggers dating from the Renaissance period – demonstrate the high level of arms production in Europe.

In the 16th century firearms were introduced and widely spread. Since then not so much the length or weight of the arms but rather the skill of the soldier determined the result of a battle or tournament. The blades became lighter, the shape of the hilt changed. It was now held by a hand wearing a more comfortable leather glove instead of steel gauntlet which had once restricted the freedom of movement. For defence short daggers were used – short thrusts were done with the left arm.

Sword. First half of the 16th century. Italy, Venice (?). Steel, silver, mother-of-pearl and precious stones; blueing and gold inlay. Length 106 cm

Glaive sword. Circa 1600–1610. Northern Italy, Venice (?). Steel; chasing, engraving, gold and silver inlay

Crossbow.
Saxony (?). Steel, wood and velvet;
engraving, gilding and ivory inlay

The sword and dagger were often fashioned by the same master and formed a set.

Crossbow, or arbalest, was a leading and most dangerous weapon employed in the 15th – 16th centuries. It consisted of a short metal bow fixed transversely on a stock and was used for shooting bolts (arrows). No less inferior to it in its destructiveness was the glaive sword, a pole-arm consisting of a single-edged blade on the end of a pole. It was used for stabbing and cutting and would have a small hook on the reverse side to be more destructive and to catch the enemy's weapon.

In the Renaissance period items produced by famous armourers of Italy, Spain and Germany were considered objects of luxury and works of applied art.

Travelling carbine. 1650–1660. Workshop of Cominazzo and Picci. Northern Italy, Gardone-Brescia. Steel and wood; chasing and engraving

Pistol. Circa 1570. Germany, Braunschweig. Steel; chasing and engraving

Pistol. 1580–1590. Germany, Augsburg. Steel; chasing and engraving

Art of Antiquity

FIRST FLOOR: ROOMS 101, 102, 106–117, 121, 127–131

The first-floor rooms of the New Hermitage contain the collection of the art of Antiquity. Large and rich, it is sometimes uneven in the quality of the items. Most noteworthy are Roman portrait and decorative sculpture, antique gems, painted pottery and gold objects discovered in the barrows of the Northern Black Sea littoral which was once the site of many Ancient Greek colonies.

The first sculptures dating from the age of Classical Antiquity, including the famous statue *Venus of Tauride*, arrived in Russia in the reign of Peter I who intended to use most of them for the decoration of the Summer Gardens located in the centre of his new capital. However, only a small part of them proved to be genuine antique works which later found their way to the Hermitage. Catherine the Great had her own preferences. She was infatuated with antique carved stones. The core of this collection was formed by the acquisitions made personally by the empress in the 1780s for her Cabinet of Antiquities that stored products of the glyptic arts of Antiquity, numbering 10, 000 items. In 1814 the imposing perfect Gonzaga Cameo presented to Emperor Alexander I by Josephine de Beauharnais was added to the collection.

In 1861 the largest and most valuable assemblage of works from Antiquity in the entire history of the Hermitage was purchased in Rome. It included about one hundred statues, among them the statue of Jupiter, the chief god of the Roman pantheon, and the representation of Emperor Octavian Augustus on the throne. More than five hundred vases were bought; the highlights were painted Greek and Italic vessels, such as the Regina Vasorum and the famous pelike featuring a swallow, a doubtless masterpiece of the Hermitage collection of ancient pottery which comprises up to 15, 000 objects. In the enormous majestic Jupiter Hall displayed next to the statue of the god to whom the hall is dedicated are fine specimens of Roman portrait sculpture dating from the 2nd and 3rd centuries AD, the period of the flourishing of Roman sculpture that precedes the fall of the Roman Empire.

◀ **Exhibition of the Art of Antiquity.**
Twenty-Column Hall

Red–figure psykter: *Feasting Hetaerae.*
Late 6th century BC. Attica. By master Euphronios.
Clay; painting. Height 35.5 cm

This psykter used for cooling wine is signed by one of the best-known masters of the early (also called "austere") red-figure style.

The artist chose as his subject a cheerful feast of four hetaerae. The name of each girl is written in purple near her image. One of the hetaerae plays *kattab*, a fascinating love game. With a cup rotated on her finger, she is throwing a drop of wine at a mark in dedication to her beloved.

Lekythos in the form of a sphinx.
Late 5th century BC. Attica. Clay; painting
and gilding. Height 21.5 cm

It is a true masterpiece of Ancient Greek pottery in the Hermitage collection. The vessel for olive oil shaped as a sphinx with the head of a gold-haired beautiful Greek woman was found in the burial of a woman near Thanagoria (Taman Peninsula).

Kantharos shaped as a double-faced female head. 490–480 BC. Attica. By the Group of London Painter. Clay; painting. Height 17.7 cm

This is a very well-preserved red-figure vessel, with two handles, for drinking wine. It is composed of two female heads with different hairstyles. The type of the faces having well-proportioned harmonious features is in tune with the Classical ideal of beauty. The broad brim of the vessel looks like a headdress.

White–ground lekythos: *Artemis with a Swan.*
Early 5th century BC. Attica. By the Pan Painter.
Clay; painting. Height 38 cm

This flask for aromatic oil is highly interesting, as all white-ground lekythoi are. These lekythoi dating from the earlier period were provided with a strong, almost glossy "enamel-like" background on which traditional black-lacquer representations were placed. Their upper part continued to be painted in the red-figure manner.

Hydria with a scene from Eleusinian mysteries: Regina Vasorum. 4th century BC. Campania. Clay; reliefs and painting. Height 65.5 cm

It is the most notable example of the Ancient Greek pottery from the 4th century BC in the Hermitage collection. It got its honourable name of the "Queen of Vases" (Regina Vasorum) in the 19th century. This hydria was manufactured in a region of "Great Greece" (as the Greeks named their colonies in the fertile and rich Italy).

Red-figure pelike: *The First Swallow.* Second half of the 6th century BC. Attica. Clay; painting. Height 37.5 cm

One of most impressive pieces is the famous pelike made by one of the best vase painters working in the red-figure manner. The body of the vessel shows two scenes — fighting wrestlers and a conversation of three Greeks — a man, a youth and a boy. The inscriptions indicate what each of them says. "Have a look, this is a swallow!" — says the youth pointing to the bird with his finger. The bearded man raises his head: "Yes, I swear by Hercules!" — "Here it is, spring has come!" — exclaims the boy seated nearby.

Krater: *Gygantomachy.* 4th century BC. Apulia. Circle of Lycurgus. Clay; painting, black lacquer. Height 105 cm

Large red-figure kraters produced at Apulian workshops would have served as tomb stones on the graves of local nobility. Such vases differ from vessels produced by Athenian potters in their large dimensions and the emphasized sumptuousness of decorative elements. Apulian artists widely used the added white paint, the effects of light-and-shade modelling and foreshortened depictions in their red-figure paintings.

The composition on the Hermitage krater is based on the myth of the battle of the Olympian gods and giants.

Portrait of Ptolemy II and Arsinoe II
(Gonzaga Cameo). 3rd century BC. Alexandria.
Sardonyx; carving. 15.7 x 11.8 cm

The pride of the Hermitage is its collection of ancient carved gems. They are divided into two types: gems with recessed design – intaglios and relief designs – cameos. Before the campaigns of Alexander the Great many-layered sardonyx had not been available to the Greeks and this prevented them from producing cameos. However, their production flowered during the Hellenistic period. Skilfully employing layers of stone, the carver could create an illusion of light-and-shade effect. The famous Gonzaga Cameo features Ptolemy II of Egypt and his wife Arsinoe. The story of the Gonzaga Cameo is full of unusual reversals of fortune. From the collection of the Mantuan dukes it passed to Prague, then the Swedes took it to Stockholm. Christina who resigned the throne and became a Catholic, returned the cameo to Italy. Then it was bought for the Vatican, but later appeared in France. Eventually, Josephine de Beauharnais presented the cameo to the Russian emperor.

Girl with a Jug. 3rd century BC. Tanagra

The Hermitage owns a fine collection of terracotta (burnt clay) statuettes. They were used in Greece since time immemorial for private worship and for donations to temples. Female images were especially popular. The word *kore* (girl) gave its name to the art of clay sculpture in some languages. Terracotta pieces were produced in various centres of the Hellenistic world from Italy to Syria, but the figurines from the Boeotian town of Tanagra became especially numerous and fashionable.

Reclining Youth. Early 4th century. Etruria.
Bronze. Height 42 cm, base: 69.5 x 23 cm

The Hermitage collection of Etruscan antiquities is varied and contains a number of genuine masterpieces. The urn lid shaped as a youth taking part in a funerary meal manifests main features of Etruscan art: meticulous rendering of details and some neglect of the proportions which allows attaining greater expressiveness.

Aphrodite (Venus of Tauride). 1st century. Copy of the original dating from the 3rd century BC. Ancient Rome. Marble. Height 167 cm

The statue belongs to a group of works made after the originals of the great Ancient Greek artist Praxiteles who was the first to show the goddess of love and beauty naked. Aphrodite with the elongated proportions of her body and a small head crowing the long slender neck embodies the Hellenistic ideal of feminine beauty.

This first ancient statue to appear in Russia was acquired in Italy on the commission of Peter the Great who wanted to decorate his Summer Gardens with genuine pieces of antique sculpture. The statue was so highly valued that it took the art dealers a few years to convince the Italians to sell it to the Russian emperor. At first Venus was placed in an open pavilion in the Summer Gardens, later it was transferred to the palace of Prince Potemkin of Tauride, hence it received its name.

Statue of Emperor Octavian Augustus shown as Jupiter. 1st century. Ancient Rome. Marble. Height 187 cm

This statue was created after the death of Octavian (reigned 31 BC – 14 AD). The worship of the emperor began even during the lifetime of Octavian (he was awarded the title of Augustus: the Holy, divine Son, father of the native land, descendant of Venus and Aeneas), and under his successors this became an official cult. The composition was adapted from the celebrated sculpture of Zeus by Phidias, a famous Ancient Greek artist active in the 6th century BC, which allowed the placing of the appropriate attributes in Augustus's hands when the statue was restored.

Sarcophagus with a wedding scene. 3rd century.
Ancient Rome. Marble. Height 116 cm

The sarcophagus was made for the burial of a noble Roman. Such sarcophagi are called biographical, although in fact they were intended not so much to depict concrete events as to sing the praises of the main Roman virtues – military valour, piety and harmony of family relations. The idealization of the facial features and figures betrays Greek influence. Interest in portraiture, attention to details and a certain type of composition (without spare background) are characteristic of the Roman tradition.

Statue of Jupiter.
1st century. Ancient Rome.
Marble and plaster. Height
347 cm

With the increase of their wealth the needs of the Romans in sculptural decoration of their palaces, gardens and sometimes necropolises markedly grew. It is not improbable that the huge statue of Jupiter from the villa of Domitian was modelled on *Zeus of Olympus*, the great work by the most famous sculptor Phidias, active in the 5th century BC. The marble torso of the Hermitage statue is authentic while the lost bronze details were recreated in the new times.

Portrait of a Roman Woman (Portrait of a Syrian Woman). 160–170. Ancient Rome. Marble. Height 30 cm

Portrait of Emperor Lucius Verus. Third quarter of the 2nd century. Ancient Rome. Marble. Height 76 cm

A masterpiece of Ancient Roman collection, it is probably its best female portrait. It has long been known as a portrait of a Syrian woman because of the Semitic facial features. The work of a Greek sculptor, it may have been part of a funerary statue. This woman is full of amazing charm, her mood is dominated by melancholy with a hint of skepticism, a not uncommon mixture in Roman portraits of the late 2nd century AD, when mystical oriental cults were widespread.

Portraiture from the Roman Republic period is distinguished by greater realism, sometimes even grotesque. The acquaintance with antique culture led to certain idealization. The Roman portrait developed as a result of struggle between these two tendencies and finally surpassed the highest achievements of Greek sculptors. Portrait of Lucius Verus, a co-ruler with Marcus Aurelius, is a fine example of statuary from the Antonine period (almost entire 2nd century).

Portrait of Empress Cornelia Salonina. Mid-3rd century. Ancient Rome. Marble. Height 57 cm

This is a portrait of Cornelia Salonina, the wife of Emperor Gallienus, a noble and educated man who was patron of philosophers. During Gallienus's rule there was a revival of the traditions of 2nd-century Roman psychological portraiture. The young woman's body is ideally beautiful, the face has unusual features and a complex expression, that of a woman torn by contradictions and deep suffering.

The Treasure Gallery 1
FIRST FLOOR

Several rooms on the first floor of the New Hermitage showcase the Treasure Gallery 1 exhibits. Together with priceless decorations unearthed in ancient burials, it has excellent works of mediaeval Western European and Russian jewellery and splendid ornaments made of gold and precious stones that were part of the Imperial family's treasure store in the 18th – early 20th centuries. The Hermitage collection of jewellery started to take shape in the reign of Catherine II who received an extensive "heritage" of her predecessors, Empresses Anna Ioannovna and Elizabeth Petrovna, both of whom had spent large sums of money on the acquisition of objects of luxury. Catherine followed their example and sufficiently extended the collection adding to it fine pieces of art either made on her commissions or bought specially for her at European auctions. One of the rooms in Catherine II's private quarters, known as the Diamond Room, was used for the storage of the Empress's collection. Most remarkable European jewellers and court craftsmen, including Jeremie Pauzier and Duval, fulfilled the empress's commissions fashioning snuff- and beauty-spot boxes set with diamonds, emeralds, sapphires and rubies, necklaces and earrings, pendants and bouquets. It was Pauzier who produced the gold Grand Imperial Crown adorned with 5, 000 diamonds and 75 pearls. Today it is held, together with other royal regalia, in the Russian State Diamond Fund in Moscow. The Treasure Gallery, however, boasts their miniature copies (ten times smaller than the originals) that were made by the Faberge firm for the International Exhibition in Paris in 1900 and was awarded its grand prize.

◀ **Exhibition of the Treasure Gallery 1**

Amphora. 7th century BC. Dnieper area, Chertomlyk barrow. Silver; gilding and chasing. Height 70 cm

This gorgeous amphora comes from the 19-metre-tall Chertomlyk barrow. Its decor is associated with the tripartite concept of the universe adopted by the Scythians. It is interesting enough that such an important for the understanding of Scythian mythology composition was done by a Greek craftsman.

Processional Cross of St Trudpert. Late 13th century. Upper Rhine, Strasbourg. Wood, enamel, silver, iron, glass, emeralds, sapphires and other precious and semiprecious stones; chasing and polishing. Width 52 cm; height 72 cm

The artistic and semantic centre of the cross is the representation of Jesus, the Virgin and St John. The hollows in the Saviour's body and the cavity under the miniature rock crystal cross used to contain holy relics.

Statuette: *Grinder.* Early 18th century. Saxony, Dresden. Silver, uncut diamonds, rubies, emeralds, pearls, cornelian, enamel and glass; chasing, grinding and gilding

The collection of funny silver figurines decorated with precious and semiprecious stones was purchased by Peter I in Saxony, in the workshop of Melchior Dinglinger. They are distinguished not only by their virtuoso technique but also by precise and sometimes humorous psychological characteristics of the personages.

Bouquet of Flowers. 1740s. Russia, St Petersburg. By Jeremie Pauzier. Gold, silver, diamonds, precious and semiprecious stones, glass and fabric: polishing. Height 19 cm

This is the most famous of the three bouquets by Jeremie Pauzier owned by the State Hermitage. This court jeweller exhibited great technical proficiency in creating compositions made of different types of stones. Roses fashioned of "burning" rubies and garnets were placed next to flowers made of the stones of much colder tones, such as aquamarines and sapphires. The bouquet also included tiny flowers of corals, opaque chalcedony and delicate turquoise. The slender tigereye wheat ear rises up to the 33-gram amethyst shaped as a tulip that crowns the entire composition. A special charm is enhanced by the agate fly sitting, almost unnoticeably, on a petal. Ornaments of the type were first attached to the belt or shoulder; later special vases were designed for them.

Beauty–spot box. 1750s. Russia. Gold, silver, diamonds, enamel and glass; chasing and engraving. Height 2.2 cm; diameter 4.3 cm

In the late 18th century the collecting of gold snuff-, beauty-spot and bonbonniere boxes came into fashion in Russia. Catherine II bought them abroad in large quantities, and today the Hermitage has a representative collection of items of this kind.

Miniature copy of the Imperial regalia. 1899–1900. Russia, St Petersburg. Faberge firm, by Julius Rappoport. Gold, silver, platinum, diamonds, spinel, pearls, sapphires, velvet and quartzite; casting, polishing and carving

The Faberge firm (founded by the jeweller Carl Faberge; since 1885 supplier to the Imperial court) is famous for its Easter eggs, brooches, cuff-links, animal figurines etc. They were made as costly gifts to the Imperial family's relatives from other ruling European dynasties and diplomatic presents; they were also presented to the members of the Romanov family who got married or to mark the birth of a new member of the family. The larger crown from this miniature copy of the regalia is adorned with 1, 083 cut and 2, 458 uncut diamonds; the smaller one with 64 cut and 654 uncut diamonds.

The General Staff

History and Architecture

The General Staff building (1819–1829, architect Carlo Rossi) completes the ensemble of Palace Square. Its imposing majestic facade overlooking the Winter Palace skirts Palace Square by its wings. The stately triumphal arch crowned with a monumental chariot of Glory links the two wings of the General Staff building. The arch was put up as a monument to the Russian victory in the war with Napoleon (sculptors Stepan Pimanov and Vasily Demuth-Malinovsky), so its decor is dominated by the theme of military triumph.

The left (eastern) wing of the building used to house the Ministries of Finance and of Foreign Affairs, the right one was occupied by the General Staff itself and other military institutions. The first floor of the eastern wing with its formal suite of rooms facing Palace Square was used for the offices and living quarters of the Minister of Foreign Affairs. These surviving historical interiors designed in the Classical style in the early 19th century retain their original decor. In spite of their well-devised structure and clear balanced proportions they look lavishly splendid. Today they are used for the display of new Hermitage permanent exhibitions: "The Realms of the Eagle. The Art of Empire," "Pierre Bonnard and Maurice Denis. Decorative Ensembles in the Hermitage Collection" and the Museum of the Guards.

A new period in the history of Rossi's celebrated structure, which seems to have been destined to be part of the museum complex from its very beginning, started in the 1990s when the Hermitage was given its eastern wing. The restoration that is going on now is to be completed by 2014 when the museum celebrates its 250th anniversary. In accordance with the "Greater Hermitage 20/21" project it will house collections of French art from the 19th – 20th centuries, galleries of applied art etc. The General Staff building is to become a significant part of the 21st-century Hermitage.

◀ **Palace Square. View of the General Staff building**

Dancing Hall. Large mirror plates with candelabra, sweet dishes and vases for flowers.
First quarter of the 19th century. France, Paris, workshop of Pierre-Philippe Thomire

The Realms of the Eagle. The Art of Empire

The exhibition "The Realms of the Eagle. The Art of Empire" naturally fits into the interiors created by Carlo Rossi for the private quarters of the Minister of Foreign Affairs Karl Nesselrode. It is devoted to the applied art of two leading European powers – Russia and France whose emperors Alexander I and Napoleon were in political confrontation in the early 19th century. In many European countries the eagle has long been the emblem of state power. Russia and France are not exclusions. The name of the exhibition emphasizes the artistic significance of the emblem which was employed as one of the major decorative motifs in the Empire Style period. The General Staff rooms display a rich collection of porcelain, bronzes, clocks, furniture, costumes, paintings, engravings, sculptures, arms, medals and many other items dating from the first quarter of the 19th century which have been preserved in the Hermitage storerooms and have been inaccessible to the public due to the lack of exhibition spaces.

Console table with a clock: *Cupid and Psyche.*
France, Paris, workshop of Pierre-Philippe Thomire.
Wood and bronze; chasing and gilding

Pieces from the Egyptian Service. Early 19th century. France, Sevres Porcelain Factory. Painted after designs of Dominique Vivant Denon. Overglaze painting with cobalt and sepia

Egyptian Service

The so-called Egyptian Service is an example of celebrated Sevres porcelain. It was painted after designs of Dominique Vivant Denon, Director of the Louvre in the First Empire period who had been to Egypt with the French Army. The service was presented to Alexander I by Napoleon during the meeting of the two emperors in Erfurt in 1808.

One of the most magnificent rooms in the former quarters of Minister of Foreign Affairs Karl Nesselrode, i.e. Dancing Hall, intended for balls and concerts, houses a very impressive part of the exhibition – gilded bronze works produced by the workshop of Pierre-Philippe Thomire (1751–1843), outstanding master of bronzes, leading European craftsman. Set on the tables are mirror plates with numerous candelabra, sweet dishes and sculptural groups.

Drawing Room in the apartments of Countess Maria Nesselrode

Pierre Bonnard and Maurice Denis. Decorative Ensembles in the Hermitage Collection

Paintings by French artists from the late 19th – early 20th centuries displayed in "Pierre Bonnard and Maurice Denis. Decorative Ensembles in the Hermitage Collection" exhibition match the General Staff interiors as naturally as the luxurious items designed in the Empire style that are described above. The pride of place is held by the decorative panels painted by the leading representatives of the Nabi group. The story of their creation is linked with the name of the Moscow merchant and art patron Ivan Morozov. The monumental paintings were transferred to the Hermitage in 1948 from the closed Museum of New Western Art (Moscow). For many years some of them were shown in very small rooms on the third floor of the Winter Palace where major part of the collection of French art from the 19th – early 20th centuries is displayed, while others were kept in the Hermitage storerooms. The General Staff is the first place where the entire ensemble of these panels is being exhibited.

MONUMENTAL PANELS FROM IVAN MOROZOV'S MANSION

In 1907 Ivan Morozov completed reconstruction of his mansion on Prechistenka Street in Moscow and decided that it must have a novel up-to-date decoration in tune with most daring ideas. He commissioned it to Maurice Denis, leader of the Nabis group (Hebrew "nabi" means "prophet"). In the late 1880s Denis was assisted in his work by Edouard Vuillard, Pierre Bonnard, Felix Vallotton and others. Besides their interest in painting these young intellectual artists were fond of Ancient Greek philosophy and literature. They dreamt of reviving the monumental decorative style lacking in the Impressionists' oeuvre.

Morozov commissioned Denis the *Story of Psyche*. Before sending it to Moscow the artist exhibited it at the Salon in Paris in 1908. The series of elev-

Pierre Bonnard. *The Mediterranean.* 1911. Triptych. Oil on canvas. 407 x 149 cm (left part). 407 x 152 cm (central part). 407 x 149 cm (right part)

Jean-Edouard Vuillard. *In the Room.* Oil on cardboard pasted on panel. 52 x 79 cm

Aristide Maillol.
Standing Woman.
1900. Bronze

en large-scale panels and two ornamental borders perfectly fitted into the elegant concert hall of Morozov's mansion furnished with the Art Nouveau furniture made to Denis's designs, ceramic vases and statues by the sculptor Maillol.

The success of Denis's decorative panels in Moscow provoked Morozov to have another series of paintings done for the decoration of the main staircase in his mansion, yet this time he commissioned it to Pierre Bonnard. In 1910 the artist started working on a triptych later named *The Mediterranean. Panel between Columns* (the three parts of it were to be separated from one another by semi-columns). In 1911 it was exhibited at the Paris Salon d'Autumne. Unlike stylized decorative panels by Denis, where each one is an independent composition, Bonnard's paintings form a single ensemble based on the artist's impressions of the resort of Saint-Tropez.

Maurice Denis. *Cupid in Flight is Struck by the Beauty of Psyche.* 1908–09. First panel. "Story of Psyche" series. Oil on canvas. 394 x 269.5 cm

Felix Vallotton. *Interior.* 1904. Oil on canvas. 61.5 x 56 cm

The Museum of the Guards

On 9 December 2003, the feast day of St George the Conqueror, Russia's first Museum of the Guards was opened in the newly restored interiors of the General Staff building. The Imperial Guards are believed to have been established in 1700 on the day of their founder Peter I's birthday. Though the Guards took part in many battles during the 18th century, they continued to perform their initial function of guarding the sovereign and played key role in palace coups. However, during the Napoleonic Wars the Russian Guards regained the status of the elite of Russia's Armed Forces; in the first quarter of the 19th century they included artillery, engineering units and the Guards' naval company, along with infantry and cavalry.

Standard of the Life Guards Grenadier Regiment

A separate room holds priceless memorabilia given to the Hermitage by the descendants of the Russian Guards members who live abroad. One of them is the standard of the Life Guards Grenadier Regiment which comes from London. It was presented to Vladimir Putin during his official visit to Great Britain in 2003.

Standard of the Life Guards Grenadier Regiment. 1838. Russia, St Petersburg

Tsesarevich Alexei Nikolayevich's officer uniform of His Majesty's Personal Convoy. 1910s. Russia, St Petersburg

Nicholas I's General uniform of the Hussar Regiment. Mid-19th century. Russia, St Petersburg

Bratina (loving cup) in the form of a shako. 1912. Russia, St Petersburg, Faberge firm. By Hjalmar Armfeldt

Officer casque of the Life Guards Cuirassier Regiment. 1804–09. Russia

The museum displays about 200 objects, including uniforms, weaponry, banners, regiment regalia, documents, paintings, drawings, works of applied art and coins which trace the brilliant and dramatic history of the Russian Imperial Guards. Uniforms of the Guards regiments, famous for their brilliant beauty, occupy an important section in the exhibition. Each regiment had its specific colours, decorations, headgear, etc. Portraits on display show Russian Emperors Alexander I, Nicholas I, Alexander II, Alexander III and Nicholas II wearing the Guards' uniforms as well as commanders and officers of the Guards' regiments.

Bottle stopper in the form of an officer casque of the Life Guards Grenadier Regiment. 1910s. Russia

Officer cuirass of the Cavalry Regiment. 1880s. Russia

Nicholas I's General uniform of the Preobrazhensky Life Guards Regiment. Mid-19th century. Russia, St Petersburg

The Menshikov Palace

History and Architecture

In 1981 the palace of Prince Alexander Menshikov, first governor-general of St Petersburg, located on Vasilyevsky Island became part of the Hermitage. Today it houses an exhibition dedicated to the Russian culture of Peter I's epoch. When Peter gave his favourite an empty island covered with bogs he supposed that the centre of his new capital would be developed there, and the residence of the governor, founded in 1710, was to become one of most splendid and lavish structures of St Petersburg. The palace, one of the first stone buildings in the city, completed by 1727 is a rare specimen of architecture from the first quarter of the 18th century. Its construction involved many celebrated architects invited by Peter I from Europe, such as Giovanni Mario Fontana, Johann Gottfried Schaedel, Domenico Trezzini, Georg Johann Mattarnovi, Jean-Baptiste Alexandre Le Blond.

The palace was the most luxurious building of St Petersburg in Peter's time and was often used for official diplomatic receptions and assemblies. Its main facade overlooking the Neva embankment is very impressive even today, the more so in the 18th century it struck the visitors with its size and grandeur. The palace with its central part topped with an attic, and its side projections having curved pediments with princely crowns is a fine example of Petrine Baroque architecture.

The colours of the austere and elegant facades are typical of Peter I's epoch: the tall grey gabled roof matches the yellow walls and white window frames and pilasters with carved capitals. The majestic interiors are marked by unusual variety and colourfulness. Menshikov's contemporaries admired not only the rooms but exquisite collections of paintings, sculptures, works of applied art, books, coins and medals they accommodated.

Anonymous artist. *Portrait of Alexander Menshikov.* First quarter of the 18th century

Large Chamber

When in 1727 Menshikov fell in disfavour and was exiled, his property was appropriated by the state and the palace itself was given to the First Cadet Corps (military college) which produced many outstanding figures of the 18th and early 19th centuries: the military commanders Count Pyotr

INTERIORS

The main vestibule, which serves as the main entrance from the Neva embankment, is divided into several parts by rows of white columns. It is adorned with Italian marble sculptures dating from the early 18th century and antique statues from the Hermitage stocks. The superbly lit wooden staircase leads to the first floor which used to house major formal suites and living quarters. Unfortunately the original interior of the Large Chamber has not survived but it has been completely recreated in the cause of restoration. The living quarters, partly preserved, can give a notion of the original look of the residence owned by the emperor's favourite. The rooms were decorated with marble and painted in imitation of marble, adorned with decorative painted panels, carved and inlaid wood panels, stamped leather, all sorts of fabrics and tapestries. As it is known Peter I who was fond of

Main staircase. Upper vestibule

Large (Assembly) Hall

all things Dutch set fashion for tiles. In the Menshikov Palace thirty rooms were lined with painted tiles; four of these are still extant. These are Room before the Bedchamber, Bedchamber, Study of Alexander Menshikov and Varvara's Room. Here the tiles covered not only the walls but also ceilings. No less sumptuous are rooms lined with wood panels. The walls of the Walnut Study of the prince are lined with inlaid walnut panels of various shades and divided by pilasters with gilded bronze capitals and ornamental overlays.

Rumyantsev-Zadunaysky, Count Alexander Suvorov, the dramatist and poet Alexander Sumarokov, the first Russian actor Fyodor Volkov and others. Unfortunately in the Soviet period the Menshikov Palace underwent a number of reconstructions, got dilapidated and was almost lost. The original appearance of the palace was recreated in the course of long restoration work started in the 1960s.

Walnut Study of Prince Alexander Menshikov

The Restoration
and Storage Centre

It is well known that even the largest museums can't afford displaying their entire collections in their rooms and halls; some of the exhibits have to be kept in stocks and leave them only for temporary exhibitions. That is why repositories are so important for every museum.

The Restoration and Storage Centre of the State Hermitage opened in 2003. It became a gift not only for the museum but also for the city which was celebrating its 300th anniversary at the moment. For the first time in the Hermitage history many objects which had been kept in stocks became available to the general public. Paintings, sculptures, works of applied art and archaeological finds were transferred and are still being moved here from too old and inconvenient storage spaces. The new centre is equipped with computers and up-to-date facilities providing an ideal environment for the storage of the Hermitage treasures. Its restoration workshops, auxiliary and administrative quarters are fitted with most modern devices. The Centre's priority task is preservation and study of art works, as Hermitage Director Mikhail Piotrovsky expressed it: "It is not just a storehouse but a complex 'mechanism' preserving for future generations our cultural heritage."

Though the centre is not an exhibition space, it functions according to the principle of "open storage." The tour route open to visitors extends for around one kilometer and cover all its floors. In the rooms where a certain level of temperature and humidity must be maintained, the objects can be seen by visitors from special glassed corridors. Available here are large collections and separate items which have never been exhibited before. Four more buildings are under construction now. They will house workshops for restorers, biological control laboratories and special spaces for education activities. The Hermitage Restoration and Preservation Centre is the largest in the world.

Grand Coronation Carriage. Early 1720s. France, Paris. Gobelins Tapestry Manufactory (?). Painting by Francois Boucher (?). Wood, metal, leather, velvet, horse-hair, linen and glass; carving, casting, chasing, embroidery, gilding and painting in oil. 600 x 200 x 300 cm

◀ **Storeroom of Early Russian Painting**

The Museum of Porcelain

The Museum of the celebrated Imperial Porcelain Factory is also part of the State Hermitage today. The story of its collection is inextricably linked with the story of the production of porcelain in Russia. Porcelain was actually invented in China and the composition of porcelain paste was kept in secret. In the 1740s, however, the scientist Dmitry Vinogradov, after a long session of experiments, succeeded in making porcelain paste of local raw materials that rivalled the Chinese paste in its quality. In 1756 Empress Elizabeth Petrovna commissioned her first dinner set, known as Her Majesty's Own Service. In 1765 the porcelain manufacture got the name of the Imperial Porcelain Factory. The culmination of its development was marked by the production of such ensembles as Yacht, Arabesque and Cabinet services. In 1844 Emperor Nicholas I opened a museum at the factory to mark the latter's centenary. The museum was to house best works manufactured in St Petersburg. In the reign of Alexander II the factory made copies of most unique designs which were displayed in the museum where the factory artists and modellers could study techniques and methods of their predecessors. In the Soviet period the factory was named after Mikhail Lomonosov. It continued producing works that enjoyed fame both in Russia and abroad.

In 2001 the Lomonosov Porcelain Factory museum containing over 300, 000 items received the status of Hermitage collection. In December 2003 the Museum of Porcelain fitted with up-to-date equipment was ceremoniously opened in two rooms of the factory's first floor. It showcases more than 600 exhibits. In January 2005 the factory was given back its historical name of the Imperial Porcelain Factory.

Lady with a Mask. 1906. Model by Konstantin Somov. Painted with the assistance of Somov. Porcelain; overglaze polychrome painting and gilding. Height 22.5 cm

◀ **Museum display**

Index of Names

THE STATE HERMITAGE
Guidebook

P-2 Art Publishers, St Petersburg

Производитель ЗАО «П-2»
197101, Россия, Санкт-Петербург, ул. Мира, д. 3